REMINISCING IN TRANQUILITY OF A TIME LONG GONE BY

A Sequel to Mining My Own Life

K. B. CHANDRA RAJ

Order this book online at www.trafford.com
or email orders@trafford.com

Most Trafford titles are also available at major online book retailers.

Print information available on the last page.

ISBN: 978-1-4907-7936-2 (sc)
ISBN: 978-1-4907-7938-6 (hc)
ISBN: 978-1-4907-7937-9 (e)

Library of Congress Control Number: 2017900342

Trafford rev. 01/28/2017

Trafford PUBLISHING® www.trafford.com
North America & international
toll-free: 1 888 232 4444 (USA & Canada)
fax: 812 355 4082

DEDICATION

This book is dedicated to Jeya the sister I had longed for and never had, the sister I was promised and never delivered.

May her soul be at peace and may her memory be blessed.

***Req**uiescat In **P**ace*

ACKNOWLEDGEMENT

Charles Dickens as a household name second only to Shakespeare said when he saw his first book in print he could not hold back his tears of arrant joy.

I feel the same every time I see my book in print.

Thanks to you librarian Maureen Armstrong and to your genial assistants Robert and Pat – for me you alone make it happen.

TO THE READER:

What I am doing here is to act the part of the two faced Janus – one face to look at the past and the other ahead to the future both at once; retrieve from memory without the aid of notes, events that had their genesis three score years and ten and more ago.

However much I may whip into shape my memory the undertaking sad to say is Sisyphean for I have to strenuously like the dickens strive to prevail over the inertness that inures to time and distance. Time – three score and ten plus and Distance – the theater wherein all the thrust and parry of life played out, far flung – Malaysia and Sri Lanka in South East Asia, Sierra Leone and Liberia in West Africa and the United States of America.

I must be vigilant to ensure I do not pretend to remember more than I really do - the lines of demarcation between invention and reminiscence are indistinctly drawn. It's a consummation devoutly to be wished for, distance of time and declining years trigger many doubts: "Did I really live through that?" or was I told that it happened? Or did I read about it and over the silent celerity of time believed it happened to me.

I must be watchful not to distort, falsify or prettify events. Telling a true story is a selective activity, a process of picking and choosing from a smorgasbord of experiences some while being entertaining to the readers may be embarrassing to the writer. Of his naïveté! And yet he must paying heed to his inner voice proceed to "hew the line and let the chips fall where they may."

I felt queasy writing about color and caste. Coerced by my conscience to be truthful, "to hold as 'twere the mirror up to nature, to show virtue her feature, scorn her own image" I deemed it binding on me to call the attention of the reader to the ugly faces of color (universally) and caste (locally) though forever staring at us, we adopt for civility's sake an attitude of contrived blindness.

1. What you will find in this narrative is brief episodes and casual encounters I reflect on from the secure perch of old age what psychiatrist and author Robert Jay Lifton calls "Retirement Wisdom." These recollections do not come in single file like soldiers marching in lockstep on the orders of the Sergeant Major.

2. This book is a sequel to "Mining My Own Life." Friends who have read this book must feel they know me through and through, as if seen me naked without my consent.

3. L'espirit de l' escalier or 'wit of the stair case.' It often happens an apt and witty riposte occurs after the "assailant" has departed. So too after I had submitted my manuscript to the publishers many incidents I realized that merited mention had been passed over. I recall Ron Howard the brilliant director of the film "Da Vinci Code" once remarking that most times it is on his way home after an interview that important information that he should have provided occurs to him.

4. This book is designed to remedy this all too human lapse.

5. Susan Weidner, Mary Karr, Frank Mc Court, Sammy Davis Jr all wrote sequels, some of extraordinary length and in excruciating detail. In fact Mary Karr wrote three memoirs, the very successful "Liar's Club" was followed by "Cherry" and "Lit"

6. Drawing from memory by virtue of its anarchic nature, they do not conform to the rules of strict chronology. They come in pieces, in dribs and drabs and fits and starts that do not always fit together perfectly. I made no attempt to force them into sequence.

7. While remaining true to my memory and recording events as I remember them I make a few sallies outside the ambit of my recollections. We are not made out of wood let alone stone.

8. When one writes from his experience, everything depends on how relentlessly he forces from this experience the last drop be it sweet, bitter or sour, cynical or surly.

9. Without hurting the living or distressing the dead I have changed certain proper names.

10. Italics and highlights for emphasis are by me. I take responsibility for all errors and opinions within.

11. Caught up in the giddy frisson of having published three books I was able to stomp my way to this my fourth. As for the future I hand you over to the Bard.

"If we meet again, then we'll smile indeed.

If not, it's true this parting was well done."

Julius Caesar: Act 5. Scene1.

I do not wish to achieve immortality through my work.

I want to achieve it through not dying.

Woody Allen

It's never too late to be what you may have been

George Eliot (author of "Silas Marner")

"I sing, O muse, of a story I know

Of a Leprechaun boy just three inches low.

Grant me the words, O Gods of Green,

Sharpen my memory ever so keen,

Help me recall that tale of old,

Of wars that were fought over Leprechaun Gold,

Of a Leprechaun seeking to find a lost ring,

Who gained for himself the title of king and

Found in the end a wife to match,

So to tell the whole story I'll start from scratch."

From "The Idiot and the Oddity"

Written by David Morice while in High School

Author's supplication:

Give me O Gods of Green firmness of mind and just a "leetle" more time to complete this book of mine. Thereafter dear friends tried and true I shall with a Willy Loman shine on my sloppy –slip-on- shoes and that Puckish Gene Kelly smile on my atrophying face soldier on to the "Promised Land."

Preface

Having been notably lackluster in my grammatical studies in high school, beset by temporal myopia, eyes always preened to the playing field, not having ever taken any writing courses, or been inside of a university to me a strange undiscovered country, my life experiences working as an accountant in three continents is my Yale and Harvard my Oxford and Cambridge.

John Cheever and Raymond Carver refused to subscribe to Scot Fitzgerald's belief what some have found to be risible that "There are no second acts in American life." In golf parlance Scot Fitzgerald opines in life *you* don't get a mulligan.

If America is about anything it is about the possibility of reinventing oneself in spite of repeated mistakes and failures and setbacks. Lincoln lost eight elections, failed twice in business and suffered a nervous breakdown. Abraham Lincoln's phoenix like ascent from the ashes of defeats and disappointments should serve as our enchiridion and so steel our collective spines to soar to heights limited only by our vision and will.

Moses was eighty when he commenced his forty year walkathon to the Promised Land. Cato began studying Greek at eighty and Russian thereafter.

And Winston Churchill believed "Success consists of going from failure to failure without loss of enthusiasm." President Theodore Roosevelt in an address at the Sorbonne –

"It is not the critic who counts, not the man who points out how the strong man stumbled, or where the doer of deeds could have done better. The credit belongs to the man who is actually in the arena, whose face is marred by the dust and sweat and blood; who strives valiantly; who errs; *and comes short again and again; because there is no effort without error or shortcoming*; who knows the great enthusiasms, the great devotions and spends himself in a worthy cause; who, at the best, knows *in the end the triumph of high achievement, and who**, at worst, if he fails, at least fails while daring greatly."***

".. at worst, If he fails, at least fails, while daring greatly." So be it with this book my fourth.

Those who gave Scot Fitzgerald the lie include:

Thomas Edison

Walt Disney

J.K.Rowling

Stephen King

Bill Gates

Henry Ford.

I subscribe to George Eliot's belief that "It's never too late to be what you may have been" giving short shrift to the injudicious dispiriting view that it is futile to attempt in old age what should have been done in one's juvenescence, the years of maximum receptivity.

And so like Herman Melville's elusive white whale "The Moby Dick" with harpoons embedded in its body continues to pursue and be pursued, like lonely Lawrence (of Arabia) kept on walking across the Sinai, the mountain climber who has commenced his climb without the right equipment will keep on climbing I reflect on a time long gone by, reminisce and record. Thunder must follow lightning, the mosquito will bite and I must write. Writing gives me the airs, the chops, makes me feel wiser than I am.

As Moses did I keep on looking over to the Promised Land of elegant writing from Gilead to Jericho to the Mediterranean Sea and like Moses I may not get there. Surely I have sufficient native wit to know I'll never be able to write like Cervantes, Dante and Dickens, Shakespeare, Keats or Steinbeck. The butterfly longs for the stars and dies in the fire of a candle light. Pray what parish priest would not like to be Pope; does not every foot soldier in his mind carry a Marshall's baton and every senator and governor of this blessed land salivate over the awesome power, prestige and perquisites appertaining to the presidency - the chance to throw fabulous State Dinners in honor of foreign dignitaries, to command the comings and goings of Air Force One? And yet I must keep on trying and hoping and believing. Who knows? Is it not from the irritation in the oyster the pearl is produced and from the forbidding chrysalis the beautiful butterfly emerges?

Mine has been a long and tortuous journey, highs and lows, triumphs and travails, from innocence by way of expedience to hard- won experience an experience I long to share with those I am close. There is also joy and excitement in the telling of it. The chase at times is more rewarding than the catch. I like my writing to be in style *euphonious,* in cadence *epideictic.*

For these reasons I have decided to put pen to paper or must I say fingers to the keyboard unconcerned like Charles Dickens who stated in the last line of his absorbing short story "George Silverman's Expedition" "I pen it for the relief of my own mind, not foreseeing whether or not it will ever have a reader."

What I am about to narrate is for the most part of a time, a place, even a way of life long gone. Peering into the abyss of the past, tugging back the curtain of time, when memory is cast back several decades it is likely to be imprecise like a fisherman when he casts haphazardly his net he sometimes hauls in what is irrelevant and misses what is crucial.

And so my friends before age further diminishes my recollections, before the remainder of my days is maimed, marred and rendered incomplete, before I succumb fully to these menacing signs and symptoms of "seniority" - incontinence, insomnia and (dear me) impotence, while the beauty and beastly brutality of my personal experience from the burning ground of the past to the safe tranquility of the present remains unrecorded I must go into print. Else I fear it will vanish in perpetuum.

But I say unto you. That every idle word that men shall speak, they shall give account thereof on the Day of Judgment. For by thy words thou shall be justified, and by thy words thou shall be condemned.

Mathew 12:36: 37

“THE DEAD LIVE ON IN THE MINDS OF THE LIVING”

Doris Kearns Goodwin in “Team of rivals”

The sister I longed for and never had, the sister I was promised and never delivered.

She was my father’s older brother’s daughter. She was my mother’s first cousin’s daughter. Can family blood get more viscous than this? Yes it can. My two grand mothers were sisters.

My father’s brother left Ceylon (now called Sri Lanka) and went to Federated Malay States (now Malaysia) to work in the ‘Malayan Railways.’ He had taken up residence in Taiping. My brother and I would call him “Taiping uncle” and my aunt “Taiping aunty”

It is very likely the brother found a job for my father in the Malayan Railways and that was how he ended up so far from Sandilipay a village north of Ceylon where his folks lived. My father now with the Malayan Railways would commute daily by train from Sentul a village about six-seven miles from Kuala Lumpur his work place. This he continued to do until retirement. To this day close- knit relatives refer to my parents as “Sentul uncle” and “Sentul aunty.” This was the custom in those days.

My father’s brother was a good man, a kind man, a man bereft of guile or pretensions. Not braggadocios, never boastful he would set about his chores with an impish smile which was natural and unforced. His childish chuckle would open your heart to him. My father loved him dearly, a love that was circumscribed by mutual respect and concern for each other. On important matters personal or office connected saying "let me check with Anney first" he would contact his brother for my father knew he would get the best advice a loving brother could give.

World War 11 was over. The Japs had been driven away by the Brits. Two brothers and two sisters residing in Malaysia had to take a decision that would change the contours of their lives, those of their children and their progeny for posterity. To return home or not was the vexing question. There were protracted communications back and forth between the siblings. My dad, his brother and one sister in the interests of the children's education decided to return while the remaining sister and family made Malaysia their home.

As I write this my thoughts go back many, many monsoons to the day when I visited my uncle in the hospital in Ceylon. It was the cancer hospital in Maharagama. My mother like most mothers driven by the dictum "do the right thing" said my uncle was very ill and I should pay a call. She must have known. I was taken to the room where he lay dying. He was in searing pain. Perhaps pain killers were either unknown or hard to come by in those days. Else why should he have been allowed to suffer so much? From his facial contortions I felt he was begging to be released. He had come face to face with the Grim Reaper it appeared. Reaching out to me in exasperation palpable and so pitiful I felt he was trying to tell me something like "why O' why these agonies" but no sound was audible. Have I not recalled so often this scene of hopeless suffering, which still stalks my memory?

I digress:

I have been nettling my parents that I wanted a sister but nothing in that order seemed to be happening. I was now beginning to display disturbing signs of losing patience and my mother very likely noticed this and so one day perhaps to be rid of the onerous responsibility or because of her inability to incubate a little sister for me she puts *finis* to my aching this way. "Chandra!" she says peremptorily in a tone that permitted no room for negotiation, "you can forget about your ever getting a sister. It's just not going to happen." I knew the die has been cast. For one who had been for many years fondly nursing the prospect of having a little sister, this was a bombshell bolt from out of the blue. I had a backup plan though, a second line of offense. "If that's so" whipping out my ace of spades I said with equal finality, "in that case as from now on I'll call (my father's niece) Jeya "Thangkachi"- younger sister. Jeya who was older than I became from now on the sister I had longed for and never had. The sister I was promised and not delivered. My cousin too zestfully went along with the arrangement.

Thus by celestial design a robust cosmic filial bond had been forged.

"Even before the beginning of human history, people recognized that parents transmit something – call it "likeness" – to their children, and the children to their children, and so on down the generation"

James Gleick reviewing "The Gene" by Siddhartha Mukherjee

Just as a chicken takes the shape of the egg so too Thangkachi brought to her life the fine character attributes of her father. Sanguine, tranquil, unflappable and urbane she was an oasis of peace and contentment. If she suffered inner turmoil she never showed it. Serene and focused she always got the job done. Like a duck calm and placid above water would paddle a mile a minute below she too would go about nary a fuss to meet her goals. A Sanskrit and Tamil scholar Thangkachi was pleasantly surprised one night when she visited us.

Thangkachi and I were visiting our parents in Chankanai, a village north of Ceylon. Our houses were within patting distance of each other. One night after dinner she visited us for a snap chat or to use a period slang, a "con chat". There at this family caucus was a cousin in the family way. The expectant mother quite alive to the fact that Thangkachi was a Sanskrit/ Tamil scholar requested those present to suggest a name for the baby. In a flash I said "Triveni." Visibly jolted by my suggestion Thangkachi turned round and asked me "How on earth did you come up with it. That's the best."

In Hinduism there is nothing holier than the point at which the three sacred rivers, Ganga, Yamuna and Saraswathi converge. This confluence of the three most holy rivers is called Triveni. The baby was a girl and she was named Triveni. A few years ago Triveni contacted me by e-mail. I believe she lives in the United States.

Words make their way in the world without a master, and anyone with little cleverness can appropriate them and do business with them.

Isabel Allende

There are more things in heaven and earth, Horatio, than are dreamt of in your philosophy. Hamlet (1.5. 167-8)

My wife was keen that I should visit my brother my only sibling who lives in Auckland, New Zealand and do a twofer, look up Thangkachi and close friends in Perth, Australia. By no means long in the planning one might say the undertaking was kind of autoschediastic.

On arrival in Auckland I learnt Thangkachi had been diagnosed with pancreatic cancer. The cancer had advanced to a stage where no further treatment options were available. The doctors had run out of counter measures. It was time to prepare her for the final journey, time for the family to close ranks, time to spend every denuding hours, minutes nowhere else but in her presence. She was about to take her final bow and the curtain after eight decades was about to come down.

There I was at her bedside having travelled half way round the globe to down under in Perth, Australia with absolutely no foreknowledge of her state of health to kiss her *"Auf Wiedersehen"* and god speed on her final journey after over fifty years doing the same for her dad, my dad's brother.

The will power of the dying is immeasurable, beyond mortal cognition.

On my visit she appeared to me distant and distracted. I believe she had plenty to tell me but was unable to do so. She whispered in soft tones "I am feeling weak" and to the end gracious "Thanks for coming." One felt her soul growing as her body was wasting away. She was in a transitional state in which condition the departing I have read can see persons and hear voices of the loved ones who had preceded them. To this we the living are not privy to. But there have been exceptions, chinks in the wall of separation between the living and leaving through which we are able to take a peep giving veracity to this experience.

(From "Sinatra's Century" by David Lehman)

In 1998, when he lay dying, (Frank) Sinatra had a designated thug in his room at all times. At one point Sinatra raised his head and pointed to an empty chair.

"Could you get my mother out of here?" he said. "I'm trying to get some rest, but she keeps hanging around."

Should be mentioned Sinatra's mother had a domineering influence over her son

We most often die not in the arms of those we love but in a hospital room or hospice, the florescent lights above, the blank faces of dying patients around us, away from family and familiar faces, cut off from the comforts of hearth an' home, crisscrossed by confusing wires, protruding tubes, bewildering machinery, hurrying polite but removed uniformed nurses and stunned family members beseeching the final arbiter, "Please say it ain't so"

In stating this I am supported by W. Y. Evans – Wentz for in his preface to the second edition of "The Tibetan Book of the Dead" he writes:

"As here in America, every effort is apt to be made by a materialistically inclined medical science to postpone, and thereby to interfere with, the death process. Very often the dying is not permitted to die in his or her own home, or in a normal, unperturbed mental condition when the hospital has been reached. To die in a hospital, probably while under the mind-benumbing influence of some opiate, or else under the stimulation of some drug injected into the body to enable the dying to cling to life as long as possible, cannot but be productive of a very undesirable death, as undesirable as that of a shell-shocked soldier on a battle-field. Even as the normal result of the birth-process may be aborted by malpractices, so, similarly, may the normal result of the death-process be aborted."

I saw Jeya in her home with Zen serenity composed and dignified as always watched over by a loving husband, children and grandchildren determined to stay physically, spiritually, soulfully close to her to the very end.

A few days after we departed she had gone to her eternal reward.

Ann Neumann in "The Good Death" writes:

"There is no glad death, I now know. It always hurts, both the dying and the left behind."

The sadness that will be a constant presence in the homes of those who loved Jeya will have no bottom will have no top, just circles and circles of never ending sorrow.

Leaving the world is no easier than entering it.

Thangkachi and I seldom corresponded and our meetings were few and widely spaced. As part of the exodus hot on the heels of the communal unrest in Sri Lanka like several thousands of her compatriots she had migrated to Australia and I, embarked on a nomadic journey which took my family to Sierra Leone and Liberia until we dropped anchor here in the United States. What bedazzles the mind is even though so vast amount of time and distance came between us, a subliminal feeling of mutual affection a love that passeth all definition prevailed to the very last syllable of time.

Sara Corpening in her book "Diary of a Mom" poses the question with rhetorical flourish, "*How do people make it through life without a sister?*"

True ease in writing flows from art, not chance, as those move easiest who have learned to dance.

Alexander Pope

The Complexion of Color and Caste

"As I would not be a slave so I would not be a master" - Abraham Lincoln in 1858

Before arriving in the United States I have been interested in learning about the treatment of "Blacks" in the United States. The population of the country of my birth, Malaysia, that of my parents, Sri Lanka, Sierra Leone and Liberia where I was employed for many years was homogeneous. This monolithic society in which I moved and mingled for a sizeable part of my life offered no opportunity to observe firsthand the fallout from the clash of color *id est, black and white.* I was eager to learn about the tension between Blacks and Whites that was latent in American society.

While I was living in Monrovia, Liberia (Monrovia, the capital was named after president James Monroe fifth president of the United States) during one of our Saturday lunches I recall asking our Sri Lankan friend Maha who was working for the International Monetary Fund and assigned to Liberia whose family had migrated to St. Paul's, Minnesota whether marriage between "Blacks and Whites" was commonplace. Why bring marriage you may ask. Could you not have asked do Blacks and Whites get along? No. I knew marriage is not a contract only between opposite / same, sexes. No it is a tacit acceptance or rejection by the families of two parties – that of the girl and of the boy as the case may be. For me, that is the definitive test. To my surprise he said "No, not by a long shot." How come why so? I wondered. My curiosity remained unsated. I seized every opportunity to learn firsthand about inter racial tensions and prejudices prevailing in the United States.

I was controller of the National Housing Authority a government corporation in Liberia whose mission is to build low cost housing for lower middle class Liberians. The project used to be popularly referred to as "from mats to mattresses program."

There were two black American V.S.Os (Volunteer Service Organization, an international institution working in third world countries) attached to the National Housing Authority. When one of them came to my office to have some procurements for a project approved I broached the subject of racial prejudice in the United States. For over an hour standing, refusing to sit down saying, "gota go, gota go" he frankly unloaded without malice as if in a reverie by rote the difficulties – housing, schools, the criminal justice system on and on the blacks must grapple with. How unfair I thought. How mean and heartless the whites must be. Why should it be so?

(I recall this. At the end of his disquisition he says to me, "You do not have to worry. Your people there will look after you.")

I began reading around this subject. The books I read made me, believe me bilious, my skin to crawl. I felt anger, then incredulity. They were exempli gratia - "The Measure of a Man" by Sidney Poitier, "Uncle Tom's Cabin, and "The Autobiography of Malcolm X."

Here are excerpts to put it mildly, distressing. After you have read them you will wonder whether Zoroaster, the prophet of ancient Iran, was all there when he called "Man, the most excellent and noble creature of the world, the principal and mighty work of God, Wonder of nature."

* From "The Measure of Man" by Sidney Poitier

(Sidney Poitier was the first African American to win an Academy Award for the Best Actor for his role in "Lilies of the Field)

When I was barely sixteen, still back in Miami, late one night I was stranded in a white, middle-class neighborhood. I had gone to the drycleaners in "our" part of town, only to discover that my clothes weren't yet ready. This was a major problem for me, because it was already late afternoon and I was planning to leave town the next day. The cleaners told me that I could try to pick up my stuff at the dry-cleaning plant across town. So I took the bus across town to this plant, but my clothes *still* weren't ready. Compounding the problem, by then the buses had stopped running and there I was, left high and dry and extremely out of place focused my attention on passing cars heading in the general direction of "colored town." Whenever I saw one that appeared to have black occupants, I would then - and only then – raise a hitchhiking thumb in the hope of flagging a ride. The first vehicle to stop was the unmarked police car that I had mistakenly thought to contain a black family.

I knew I was in trouble when the window on the front passenger side rolled down and the cop sitting there pointed to his right and said, "See that alley over there, boy? Get your ass up in there. Now" After a quick assessment of the situation, something inside me assumed a steadying control and I complied. The unmarked police car then rolled into the alley behind me.

There was no one else around. Whatever happened, there would be no witnesses. When I turned back around, I saw the muzzle of a revolver sticking through the open rear window on the driver's side, pointed at my head. Through that open window I could hear the dialogue inside vehicle: "What should we do with this boy?" "Find out what he's doing over here." "Should we shoot him here?" I could see that the hammer of the gun was cocked, and I was scared out of my mind – but mad too, furious at what appeared to be their need to belittle me.

I told them about taking the bus to the dry – cleaning plant, about trying to get my stuff, but the talk in the car only got meaner as the questioning intensified. The officer behind the wheel said, "Boy, if we let go, you think you can walk all the way home without looking back once?"

"Yes, sir," I replied

"Think about it now" he challenged. "Cuz if you look back, just once, we gonna shoot you. Think you can do that?"

"Yes, sir" I assured him.

"All right, you go ahead now. "We'll be right behind you."

I exited the alley, turned right onto the main street, and proceeded to walk the next fifty blocks – never once looking back. By shifting my eyes, but not my head, ever so slightly to the right, I could see that police car reflected in the plate-glass windows I passed. The cops were there, right on my tail, and there they stayed for the entire fifty blocks, until I turned the corner to the place where I was living with my relatives. At that point they sped away.

* From the "Autobiography of Malcolm X"

(*Time Magazine's Best of the Century issue named "The Autobiography of Malcolm X "one of the top ten works of nonfiction of this Century)*

"I kept close to the top of the class, though. The topmost scholastic standing, I remember, kept shifting between me, a girl named Audrey Slaugh, and a boy named Jimmy Cotton.

"It went on that way, as I became increasingly restless and disturbed through the first semester. And then one day, just about when those of us who had passed were about to move up to 8 – A, from which we would enter high school the next year, something happened which was to become the first major turning point in my life."

"Somehow, I happened to be alone in the class room with Mr. Ostrowski, my English teacher. He was a tall, rather reddish white man and he had a thick mustache. I had gotten some of my best marks under him, and he had always made me feel that he liked me. He was, as I have mentioned, a natural – born "advisor" about what you ought to read, to do, or think – about any and everything. We used to make unkind jokes about him: why was he teaching in Mason instead of somewhere else, getting for himself some of the "success in life" he kept telling us how to get?"

"I know that he probably meant well in what he happened to advise me that day. I doubt that he meant any harm. It was just in his nature as an American white man. I was one of his top students – but all he could see for me was the kind of future "in your place" that almost all white people see for black people."

"He told me, "Malcolm, you ought to be thinking about a career. Have you been giving it thought?""

"The truth is, I hadn't. I never have figured out why I told him, "Well, yes, sir, I've been thinking I'd like to be a lawyer." Lansing certainly had no Negro lawyers – or doctors either – in those days, to hold up an image I might have aspired to. All I really knew for certain was that a lawyer didn't wash dishes, as I was doing."

"Mr. Ostrowski looked surprised, I remember, and leaned back in his chair and clasped his hands behind his head. He kind of half- smiled and said, "Malcolm, one of life's first needs is for us to be realistic. Don't misunderstand me, now. We all here like you, you know that. But you've got to be realistic about being a nigger. A lawyer – that's no realistic goal for a nigger. You need to think about something you *can* be. You're good with your hands – making things. Everybody admires your carpentry shop work. Why don't you plan on carpentry? People like you as a person – you'd get all kinds of work."

"The more I thought afterwards about what he said, the more uneasy it made me. It just kept treading around in my mind."

From "Uncle Tom's Cabin" by Harriet Beecher Stowe

I had difficulty reading the classic "Uncle Tom's Cabin" by Harriet Beecher Stowe. True it is fiction but it has come to be accepted that it portrayed accurately the plight of the slaves during this period. I would put the book away and after weeks take it up again.

Husband and wife were separately sold to the highest bidder and children separated from the mother never to meet again. Dogs and cats were treated more "humanely"

(*President Lincoln referred to Harriet Beecher as the "little lady whose big book started the Great War." When Calvin Stowe negotiated "Uncle Tom's contract on his wife's behalf, he confided to the publishers that he hoped the novel would be successful enough so that his wife could buy a "good black silk dress."*)

Here's a piece of conversation between Haley and Shelby:

"Why, the fact is, Haley, Tom is an uncommon fellow; he is certainly worth that sum anywhere – steady, honest, capable, manages my whole farm like a clock."

"You mean honest as niggers go," said Haley, helping himself to a glass of brandy… "Some folks don't believe there is pious niggers, Shelby," said Haley, with a candid flourish of his hand, "but I *do.* I had a fellow, now, in this yer last lot I took to Orleans - 'twas as good as a meetin,' now, really, to hear that critter pray; and he was quite gentle and quiet like. He fetched me a good sum, too, for I bought him cheap of a man that was 'bliged to sell out; so I realized six hundred on him. Yes, I consider religion a valeyable thing in a nigger, when it's the genuine article, and no mistake."…

Here the door opened, and a small quadroon boy, between four and five years of age entered the room …

"Hulloa, Jim Crow" said Mr. Shelby, whistling, and snapping a bunch of raisins towards him, "Pick that up now!"

The child scampered, with all his little strength, after the prize, while his master laughed…

At this moment, the door was pushed gently open, and a young quadroon woman, apparently about twenty five, entered the room.

There needed only a glance from the child to her, to identify her as its mother. There was the same rich, full, dark eye, with its long lashes; the same ripples of silky black hair. The brown of her complexion gave way on the cheek of the strange to a perceptible flush, which deepened as she the gaze of the strange man fixed upon her in bold and undisguised admiration. Her dress was of the neatest possible fit, and set off to advantage her finely moulded shape; - a delicately formed hand and a trim foot and ankle were items of appearance that did not escape the quick eye of the trader, well used to run up at a glance the points of a fine female article.…

"By Jupiter," said the trader, turning to him in admiration, "there's an article, now! You might make your fortune on that ar gal in Orleans, any day. I've seen over a thousand, in my day, paid down for gals not a bit handsomer."

"I don't want to make my fortune on her" said Mr. Shelby, dryly: and, seeking to turn the conversation, he uncorked a bottle of fresh wine, and asked his companion's opinion of it.

"Capital, sir – first chop!" said the trader; then turning, and slapping his hand familiarly on Shelby's shoulder, he added –

"Come, how will you trade about the gal? – what shall I say for her, what'll you take?'

"You hypocrite, first take the plank out of your eye, and then, you will see clearly to remove the speck in your brother's eye" Mathew 7:5

A book may be compared to your neighbor; if it be good, it cannot last long; if bad, you cannot get rid of it too early.

Brooke

Is this the "The Road to Damascus?"

Psalm 90:10 pronounces, "The days of our years are three score and ten, and if by reason of strength they are four score years.." So when one rolls over into the unfamiliar world of octogenarians becoming a miser of time, as one day merges into the next barely, looking back with nostalgia and ahead with foreboding he with his backpack of broken promises, egregious acts of omission and commission, transgressions for which he is now a tuned to atone for, will set off on the road to Damascus in the hope by the grace of the almighty he will be transformed Paul like.

"An unexamined life" said Socrates "is not worth living"

I spent my childhood in Sentul, Malaysia, in Jaffna, Ceylon (now Sri Lanka) my adolescence, in Africa, young manhood and mature years and now in my old decrepit and declining years in the United States of America.

The two major communities that habit Sri Lanka, an island, once referred to as "pearl of the Indian Ocean" strategically located on the Indian Ocean shipping route between East and West until bitter communal strife a blow- up with horrendous consequences reduced it to a "tear drop" are Sinhalese and Tamils. I am a Tamil. The Tamils at this time lived predominantly in the north and east. My parents and relatives lived in the north. I write what I have observed among the Tamils living north of Sri Lanka.

There will be those who may take umbrage in what I write. In my defense I say this. These I witnessed with mine own eyes. A writer must call balls and strikes as he sees them.

It has taken me these many decades to examine my own life experience and juxtapose it with what I was learning about racial inequities, if not in law but in practice in the much advertised advanced countries particularly in the United States of America where my family and I live.

What made me want to examine my own life and the ways of my people I cannot say? Is this what they call an epiphany? Does this mean the journey to Damascus has begun? I do not profess to know.

I began my life as I no doubt end it amidst books.

Jean Paul Satre

CASTE

The "caste system" as it is referred to in the vernacular is pervasive. You are born into it and it stays with you until you die. There is no way you can shed it. As if though it was the mark of Cain. It's a ravaging plague of a tainted social system, a tattoo that cannot be wished away, a scar on the body politic, ugly like a twisted mouth. There is no ladder to climb out of it. It's baked into the culture. What is worse you pass it on to your progeny.

(In a purely Anglo Saxon society mobility is class-wise moving vertically – working class to middle class to upper middle class and having acquired enormous wealth by fair or foul means- Rockefeller was once asked by a student "Sir did you make all your millions by fair means?" and he replied "yes except the first" - to the top most rung of the totem pole – a Patrician in the mold of a Bush or a Baker.)

People from where I come from are broadly divided into upper and lower castes. The farmers called Vellalas form the upper caste. There are other castes such as the Pariahs, Pallan, Nallavans, Kusavans who are deemed to be lower than the Vellalas.

Now when I look back I feel contrite for the way the low caste men, women and children were treated. I do not know of them attending school. They grew up as a separate group, victims of endless injustice and sometimes brutality. If they anything but raised their voice the upper caste responded with rage and condescension.

In the hostel of the school I attended there was just one student who we knew to be of low caste. No one befriended him. He would go about his chores in silence and with dignity. I never once heard him raise his voice always polite, always servile. Although he lived amongst us he was not part of us. They were not only low caste they were outcast.

The low caste homes were mud huts and were fenced off that it was not possible to know what was going on behind the partition. Sometimes in the dead of night I have heard female screams and beatings by men fully charged with liquid courage. My grandmother would tell me "do not pay attention it has nothing to do with you."

Where did they get medical treatment? It is very likely they prepared a concoction of locally grown herbs. This is only a guess. I had no idea how they earned any money to buy their basic needs. We ignored the poor and vulnerable. While they in the grip and clutch of poverty eked out a living in the iron cage of hopelessness and squalor we of the soi-disant upper caste anointed by dubious notions of social entitlement lived in the golden cage, an age of privilege and affluence. So long as I lived in this environment I was completely immune and indifferent to the disparity. In Hinduism there is a blanket word that covers all sins. "It's their *karma,*" cosmic comeuppance in which we have no part. This way we dodge responsibility. What is breathtaking in all this is those of the low caste accepted their situation with scarcely a protest. Aldous Huxley in "The Brave New World" explains it this way. "Most men and women will grow up to love their servitude and never dream of revolution." So it was with the depressed castes, the uncomplaining uncared for poor in my home town.

They were not allowed to enter the homes of the upper caste. (*Under slavery in the United States the "House Niggers" superficially at least were part of the household.)* They tramped bare bodied and barefooted. One pariah, his name was Poothan would come to our home and my father enjoyed talking to him. He would sit on the ground outside the house and my father seated in the veranda smoking a cheroot would carry on a conversation. Poothan would sometimes visit with his little son. The son would sit by the father's side on the ground. One day the little fella came running into and on to the veranda where my father was seated. The father of the lad promptly jumped into action. Apologizing, the father dragged the lad out saying "You know you should not go in" gave the little blighter a sound tongue lashing. Witnessing this how did I react? I did not see anything wrong. I was completely insensitive to the feelings of the child or the father. There was no moral conflict, guilt or sense of sin. I would go further and say our collective consciences were muted.

Those of the low caste "the untouchables" could not eat in the boutiques of the upper caste. Before I was admitted to the school hostel for a couple of weeks I commuted by bullock cart, the equivalent of horse and trap. I would wait for my "transport" within the precincts of a tea boutique and on sighting the "carrier" would run over to hop on to it. It was a week after I had come from Malaysia to settle down in the northern part of Ceylon. Word had got around. My grandmother said to me I should not stand there for my ride. No reason was given. This was a time when parents and grandparents never gave reasons. I later learnt the boutique belonged to an untouchable low caste. No attempt in any significant way was made to protect the feeble. On the contrary no opportunity was missed to oppress them. Underneath the supposed civilized veneer of "high caste", "upper crust" Tamil *Homo Sapiens* there lurked an insensitivity that was *par for the course.*

If "Jim Crow" was a way of life, so was the caste system; if "Uncle Tom" describes an excessively servile person then we had our "Uncle Toms" too in the human forms of Pariahs and Pallans. The white identity needs a black identity in order to define itself. So too the upper caste needed a lower caste. We all have the innate need to feel superior to someone. Times without number I have been accosted by one on whom I have not laid eyes before with the question "Where are you from?" which to me smacks of condescension. Said Lyndon B. Johnson who signed the Civil Rights Act on July 02, 1964,

"If you can convince the lowest white man he's better than the best colored man, he won't notice you're picking his pocket. Hell, give him somebody to look down on, and he'll empty his pocket for you."

Even affluent low caste families (there were few) could not buy houses in high caste neighborhoods. (*When my brother's house was about to be sold to a "low caste" bidder couple of years ago it was grabbed by the same "high caste" individual who was haggling over the price.*) Wisely low caste folks who could afford it moved away to the metropolis where they could mingle with the rest unrecognized. While with righteous indignation we protested in the streets against apartheid in South Africa we were fostering it in our backyard without a twinge of conscience.

Those of the low caste were forbidden from entering Hindu temples for worship. They would stand at a distance, outside the confines and pray while those of the upper caste worshiped from within the building. The counter argument by the "upper caste" folks was that they were not permitted near the "Moolasthanam" the sacred area from where the priest performed the rituals none of us understood. So what are they complaining was the refrain?

My father in law was the governing director of a temple and he created a sensation a revolution in fact by throwing open the temple doors to all. In the little caste ridden world of northern Sri Lanka he was an *abolitionist,* cast in the mold of Frederick Douglas, Harriet Beecher Stowe and Harriet Tubman. He was not ahead of his time. He was on time. It is we who were late and sadly still are.

The caste system is so reviled that racial hatred and discrimination is referred to as racial caste. In her book, "The New Jim Crow" Michelle Alexander the highly acclaimed civil rights lawyer, advocate and legal scholar states, "We have not ended **racial caste** in America we have merely redesigned it."

The "caste system", the bed rock on which the Tamil Hindu society in the north of Sri Lanka is built upon has come to represent a phenomenon, in fact a way of life that is reprehensible and must be distanced. The "caste system" as an expression has found safe harbor in the English lexicon can be evidenced from the front page report in the Sunday New York Times of April 24, 2016.

"In the New Age of privilege not all are in the Same Boat. Marketing to rich customers, companies foster a money-based **caste system.**"

Harriet Beecher Stowe in "Uncle Tom's Cabin" provides us the tape by which we can measure the righteousness or otherwise of our actions. "There is one thing that every individual can do, - they can see to it that they feel right."

And in Hamlet Polonius to his son on the eve of his departure to France,

"This above all- to thine own self be true
And it must follow, as the night the day
Thou canst then be false to any man."

Mahatma Gandhi moved to pity by the plight of those of the low caste would refer to them as "*Harijans*" which means "children of God." Harijan, low caste, depressed caste made no difference. French fries or Freedom fries the color, content and crispiness is the same. The upper caste though not necessarily always upper crust believed a pariah by any other name was just as bad. The high hat attitude of the upper caste remained undeviating.

The Tamil Christians regardless to what caste they belonged were allowed to enter churches for worship. The Tamils who became Christians had access to good schools and therefore better education. The Christian missionaries when converting the Tamil Hindus gave them English names. Manickam and Muthiah were told henceforth you are Mather and Mills and Appiah was baptized Arnold. Consequently after a period it was not possible to state with certainty to what caste the Tamil Christians with English names originally belonged. This was one way a low caste Tamil could rid the stigma of caste.

There was another distinction with a big difference between the names of Tamil Hindus and Tamil Christians. A Sanders's son would always go as Sanders. A Tamil Sanders in New Zealand will very likely be related to a Tamil Sanders in Timbuktu. Hindus went by their given names. Kandiah's son Suppiah would go as K.Suppiah and his son Moorthy would be known as S. Moorthy. This practice was peculiar only among the Tamils. The Sinhalese be they Christians or Buddhists retained the same surname, names which had their well spring in Portuguese and Dutch sources. Names like De Silva, Fernando and Perera. It is my observation superficial though it may be that like Tamil Hindus many Sinhalese Buddhists did not trade- in their original family name like Amunugama, Ariadasa and Aravinda for Portuguese and Dutch names in vogue.

It must be mentioned not all Tamil converts to Christianity assumed English names.

Did not Saul on the road to Damascus dust away his Roman name and become Paul? Was not Simon renamed Petra (Peter)?

(*My friend T. (T. for Thiagarajah) Vel Murugan meaning the Hindu God Murugan with the trident said to me wistfully while we were on an audit that on his first day at a prominent Christian school in Colombo Sri Lanka, the class teacher refused to register his name unless he changed it. He complied. Changed his name to V.M.Thiagarajah. There are times in one's life it is wise to promptly pocket your pride and proceed without losing sight of your game plan.*

Nations like slaves change names on gaining independence from their colonial masters. Ghana was once called Gold Coast and the euphonious Serendipity was toned down to Ceylon in colonial times and in a surge of patriotic nativism has been renamed in the vernacular - Sri Lanka.

Like the few Christian Tamils blessed with inner conviction and comfortable in their skin held on to their birth names rather than barter it for a brand new one at baptism, Sierra Leone and Liberia where we lived for many years felt no need for a cosmetic makeover.

Shedding the one inherited at birth and donning a new faith is as old as time. The poet John Donne ("No Man is an island" and "Death be not proud") converted to Protestantism, the faith of his patrons, because his vertical progression as a priest was in that profession. Born Jewish savage German anti-Semitism drove Edith Stein to become a Catholic nun. Cassius Marcellus Clay Jr drawn to black Muslims' feelings of racial pride chose to become Muhammad Ali. Submitting to the gentle coercion of convenience with a view to making social life less complicated one takes up the faith of the spouse.

(Many years ago while working in New York City a Jewish colleague by the name Anton Berlin said to me when his father fled Germany under Hitler on his arrival in London changed his name to Berlin)

For the most part Jews who changed their names however (Lawrence Zeigler to Larry King, Jonathan Leibowitz to Jon Stewart and Krinsky to (Michael) Kinsley remained loyal to their faith.

(On the subject of changing names this incident comes to mind. At the last meeting with the immigration official before he signed me off for citizenship he said this is the time to change my name if I so desired. "Give me a minute" I said and dashed off to my wife seated in the hall and asked what she thought about it. Always on the qui vive she said, "This is the name given by our parents why change it" and thus

my name "Chan dra ra ra"- as my friends here in the U S.A would cavalierly enunciate it - was soldered to my soul.)

Over time the lives of Tamil Hindus and those of Tamil Christians divaricated. They lived within their own circles, circles that almost never intersected except transactionally. The Tamil Christians with the injection of funds and financial backing from Christian missionaries and scholarships to schools became better educated, fluent in English, westernized in their ways and more accommodating of the stigma and baggage caste brings with it.

Tamils were a minority and Tamil Christians were now relegated to a position of being a minority within a minority with its attending insecurities. And so a perceptible special bond among Tamil Christians was born. Christian homes were mostly within walking distance of schools and churches. A smart uncle of mine, a Hindu who would have accredited himself with honors scholastically could not proceed beyond high school diploma; had to enter government service as his parents did not have the wherewithal. Tamil Hindus proudly holding stead-fast to their traditions and customs hallowed by time handed down from sire to son, smug and complacent with delusions of superiority lagged behind.

Being caste conscious, Tamil Hindus often married within the family and all too often from the same village as was the case of my parents. This way they made certain the purity of their caste remained unadulterated even if this meant inbreeding with all its genetic downside. Since caste was no big deal Christians were relatively more liberal in their choice of spouses.

While low caste Tamils lived in ghettos the Tamil Hindus and, Tamil Christians in the proximity of school and church, lived in reservations of their own making and choice.

Marriage between Tamil Hindus and Tamil Christians (you could say the same for cross marriages between Tamils and Sinhalese) was an embarrassing novelty. Unwanted by the Hindus and uncared for by the Christians this new "breed" became the Jaffna man's "Ugly Duckling." Among these social misfits those professionally qualified hurriedly sought employment outside Sri Lanka and migrated mostly to the United Kingdom to begin life anew unencumbered by the social mores and cultural constrictions of their past. With the passage of time their off springs like Hans Christian Anderson's "Ugly Duckling" "became a beautiful swan, the most beautiful bird of all", the pride and prize of their progeny, the envy of those they left behind.

Man invented language to satisfy his deepened need to complain

Lily Tomlin

Kinds of Tamils in Sri Lanka

Jaffna Tamils

These are the *Bhoomi Putras* (sons of the soil) the model minority. They are children born, grew up and went to Christian schools such as Jaffna College, St. Johns, and St. Patrick's, Uduvil and Vembadi for girls in the northern part of Sri Lanka – the Jaffna peninsula. Parents and near relatives live in Jaffna. Majority of the young ones are employed in the capital city Colombo or the suburbs and during vacation they take the train to Jaffna to visit elderly parents, attend weddings and funerals.

Colombo Tamils

Boys and girls born and raised in Colombo or in its suburbs; would have attended Christian schools like St. Thomas, St. Josephs, St. Benedicts, Ladies, St. Bridget's and Methodist for girls and non-denominational Royal College.

Batticaloa Tamils and Trincomalee Tamils

Children born and living in either of these provinces. I have not visited these provinces and am not familiar with the activities in these parts. I have not known of prominent schools in these areas. Children keen on studies find their way to Colombo I would guess. They are barring exceptions of course not noted for their scholastic attainments.

I am aware there is not much interaction between Jaffna Tamils and Trincomalee/Batticaloa Tamils.

Language cannot do justice to the horror of experience but it's the only game in town and so we make the most of it.

Stone will perish, the word will remain.

Vincent Van Goh

COLOR

Once a year in January the Stentorian voice of Martin Luther King Jr will boom from every television in every home:

"I have a dream that my four little children will one day live in a nation where they will be judged not by the color of their skin but by the content of their character."

Dream on Doctor, Dream on!

Our driver Sorie in Freetown, Sierra Leone (West Africa), noir to the bone, darker than the spaces between the stars, who even when it is raining cats and dogs would, wearing a trench coat wash the car has on several occasions said to me (mind you by an African in Africa a young lad who had never left the village of his birth) "Master" and touching his forearm "this color is no good." He it appears said a gobful.

To the color black everything unpleasant and disagreeable is attributed. "Black Hole"; "Black Market"; "Black Mail"; "Black Sheep"; "Black Humor", "Black ball", except (a comic once said) the toilet roll.

(In the United States artful attempts have been made to "whitewash" the stigma that accompanies blackness. So we now call them "people of color", "persons of color" and in the Gandhi fashion of referring to low caste folks as "Harijans" Martin Luther King preferred to call them "citizens of color" It makes no difference whether we call a used

car pre owned or the prince of all tortures waterboarding, "enhanced interrogation")

As always Shakespeare has the last word – "What's in a name?"

Shakespeare is as guilty. He appears to have elicited joy from it. Othello convinced, albeit incorrectly of Desdemona's infidelity strangles her and then noticing she is not quite dead smothers her a little more to make doubly certain. Othello "happens" to be black.

In Merchant of Venice, where Shakespeare uses the assumption of Jewish vice in Shylock to create a radiant picture of Christian virtue, suitors compete for the hand of Portia. There are three caskets - made of gold, silver and lead. One casket holds the portrait of Portia. Portia must marry any suitor who picks the casket containing her portrait.

The Prince of Morocco dark of complexion arrives and wishes to try his luck. His color is recognized as a natural barrier, and an unwelcome suitor to Portia. Portia is alarmed and anxious for if this black man should choose the right casket she has to marry him.

(*In Shakespeare's day, black men like Othello and Aaron the Moor were associated with the devil and evil in general*)

The Prince points to the golden casket to find it does not have the portrait of Portia. Portia mighty relieved remarks:

"A gentle riddance; draw the curtains go,

Let all of his complexion choose me so."

In 1596 *Queen Elizabeth* 1 *called for the expulsion of black Moors from London, because there were too many of them. Reverberations of Donald Trump?*

Eye witnesses die; the written word lives forever

Anna Quindlen

Oprah Winfrey's foray into the complex world of color

Oprah today is undeniably among the richest around. Through the Oprah Winfrey Leadership Academy in Johannesburg Oprah we could say "owns" a little bit of South Africa.

While in Zurich, Switzerland for Tina Turner's wedding she walked into a shop and a hand bag behind the counter caught her fancy. The hand bag cost $40,000.00. Oprah asked to see it and this is what she was told.

"No it's too expensive."

Here we see in conflict - the color of Oprah's skin and the content of the shop assistant's character.

Dream on Doctor King Dream on - We shall overcome. Someday! May be! Readers may question how then was a black man elected twice president of the United States of America? I say it's an aberration, a onetime wonder. As writer George Will noted "In Obama the man and the moment have met." I dare say a repetition of which would be a long time coming.

Literature's most precious gift is to teach us to be alone with ourselves

Harold Bloom

The Color Bar Back Home

When a child is born in our village in Sri Lanka neighbors, all "high caste" would come over in droves to see the new born. The preference runs like this. A boy is preferred to a girl. If girl she better be light of complexion. Parents have enormous difficulty in "marrying off" a dark girl and the beleaguered father in negotiating the amount of dowry has to keep upping the ante. Author Alice Walker has coined a new word for discrimination against individuals with a dark skin tone among people of the same racial and / or ethnic groups. She calls it "colorism." It is also referred to as "Internalized Racism."

Color figures prominently in the business transaction of child adoption. Sri Lankan Tamils for reasons of cultural and linguistic affinity look to South India as the ideal farm. Parents who put a child up for adoption will not part with a boy for he is a potential source of income and as for a girl only darkies are dispensable.

It was disclosed on 2/17/2016 in a Public Policy Polling among all Republican voters in South Carolina one in ten South Carolinian Republicans is willing to openly admit that they think white people are a superior race.

Nicholas Kristof in "The New York Times" of April 3, 2016.

"One indication of how deeply rooted biases are: A rigorous study by economists found that even N.B.A. referees were more likely to call fouls on players of another race. Something similar happens in baseball,

with researches finding that umpires calling strikes are biased against black pitchers"

"In one study by scholars at Portland State University and the University of Arizona, three black men and three white men played pedestrians trying to cross a street at a cross walk. On average, a black pedestrian was passed by twice as many vehicles before a driver yielded."

Nicholas Kristof in "The New York Times" of Sunday October 2, 2016.

There are many who believe with evangelical fervor white is right white cannot be wrong if it is brown flush it down.

Sadly, casting a "Nelsonian Eye" towards racial inequity and skin pigmentation prejudice is ubiquitous and in the light of present day ideals, incongruous.

Herman Melville in "Moby Dick"

Herman Melville in "Moby Dick" which is about the pursuit of the white whale extols the color white giving it historical context. (*Italics by author*)

"Though in many natural objects, whiteness *refiningly enhances beauty,* as if imparting some special virtue of its own, as in marbles, japonicas, and pearls; and though various nations have in some way recognized a certain royal pre-eminence in this hue; even the barbaric, grand old kings of Pegu placing the title 'Lord of the White Elephants' above all their other magniloquent ascriptions of dominion; and the modern kings of Siam unfurling the same snow-white quadruped figure of a snow-white charger; and the great Austrian Empire, Caesarian, heir to over lording Rome, having for the imperial color the same imperial hue; and though this pre-eminence in it applies to the human race itself, *giving the white man ideal mastership over every dusky tribe*; and though, besides all this, whiteness has been even made significant of gladness, for *among the Romans a white stone marked a joyful day*, and though in other mortal sympathies and *symbolisings, this* same hue is made the emblem of many touching, noble things – *the innocence of brides, the benignity of age,* though among the Red Men of America the giving of the white belt of wampum was the deepest pledge of honor; though in many climes, *whiteness typifies the majesty of Justice* in the ermine of the Judge, and contributes to the daily state of kings and queens drawn by milk – white steeds; though *even in the higher mysteries of the most august religions it has been made the symbol of the divine spotlessness and power;* by the Persian fire worshippers, *the white forked flame being held the holiest on the altar;* and in the Greek mythologies, Great Jove himself being made incarnate in a snow-white bull; and though to the noble Iroquois, the midwinter sacrifice of the sacred White dog was by far the holiest festival of their theology, that spotless, faithful creature being held the purest envoy they could send to the Great Spirit with the annual tidings of their own fidelity; and though directly from the Latin word for white, all Christian priests derive the name of one part of their sacred vesture, the alb or tunic, worn beneath the cassock; and though among the holy pomps of the Romish faith, *white is specially employed in the celebration of the Passion of our Lord*: though in the Vision of St. John, *white robes are given to the redeemed, and the four and –and-twenty elders stand clothed in white* before the great white throne, and the Holy One that sitteth there white like wool; yet for all these accumulated associations, with whatever is sweet, and honorable, and sublime, there yet lurks an elusive something in the innermost idea of this hue, which strikes more of panic to the soul than that redness which affrights in blood."

Things to avoid are vagueness, hackneyed phrases, dead metaphors and decorative adjectives.

George Orwell

Color Bar on "My Door Step"

I have squirreled through books, Herman Melville's "Moby Dick" Shakespeare's "Merchant of Venice" and "Othello", related the experience of Oprah Winfrey and the preference of light to dark skin in Sri Lanka where I grew up all the time with ostrich oblivion glibly unaware that right "on my door step" there it is ominously staring at me.

I occupy an apartment in a condominium complex of seventy units where my neighbors are black, white, brown and yellow. I live in a town where the residents are black, white, brown and yellow. I am a regular visitor to the public library where I see black, white, brown and yellow patrons zestfully and amicably enjoying the facilities being provided.

But then at the time of my writing, when I scan the staff from top to toe, serving front and back, upstairs and downstairs, be it menial or managerial or the middlings in the middle, it's all monochrome as far as these feeble eyes can behold. In the changing demographical composition, an America becoming blacker and browner by the day, to the unjaundiced eye of a patron it does not appear copacetic at all.

Is it an oversight? Is it by design? Is it unavoidable? The writer has no way of knowing.

Choose the words that surprise me, use metaphors I've never heard before and avoid clichés.

Sebastian Junger – Author of "Perfect Storm"

Slave labor

While I lived in Freetown, Sierra Leone and in Monrovia, Liberia I would be told stories of how the white man with the help of natives laid traps, caught unsuspecting fellow countrymen and shipped them off to North America to work as slaves in the plantations under inhumane conditions.

The fore fathers of the then president of Liberia- we lived in one of his nephew's many apartments - was the intermediary for these well rewarded foul deeds. The treatment of African slaves in America is too well known and does not bear repetition.

Sri Lanka was not to be left out. The British who ruled Ceylon for a good many years brought Tamil speaking Indians from South India, housed them in foul, sub human conditions and worked them to the bone on tea plantations in the south of Ceylon. They were referred to as "indentured labor" whereas in fact it was indentured servitude. Certain days of the month they were not paid for their work. The tea plucker would tell his wife "Nalaikku Summa" meaning tomorrow I will not be paid.

Sri Lankans took no notice of them or the conditions in which they lived and worked. We sat quietly and countenanced the injustice. When Ceylon became independent and the natives gained the right to vote, the tea pluckers were left out although they had lived for decades in Ceylon and contributed to the prosperity of the country.

SLAVE ISLAND IN SRI LANKA

As perhaps a constant reproach to Sri Lankans' blasé attitude towards inhumanity to fellow and foreign human beings there is in the nerve center and commercial hub of the capital Colombo an area called "Slave Island" which the Portuguese and the Dutch used as transit stations for slaves transported between Africa and Europe. For countless years I have motored through this town and never once paused to inquire how it got the name "Slave Island." Recently I inquired from patriotic Sri Lankans au courant on matters appertaining to Sri Lanka and they too were none the wiser.

As always Google is next to God.

"Slave Island is a suburb in Colombo, Sri Lanka located directly south of the Fort area of Colombo. The name Slave Island was given during the period of British occupation and administration, and refers to the situation under Portuguese and Dutch administrations when slaves were held there, most of them from Africa."

Here's what Yaa Gyasi, author of "Homecoming" writes on the same subject.

"I went to Ghana the summer after my sophomore year at Stanford to research a novel. I'd arrived with a different novel in mind. But when I first stepped into the Cape Coast Castle, a place where slaves were confined before being shipped to the New World, a place just fifty miles from the town where my mother grew up, I couldn't believe that my family had never talked about it.

I thought of how we were so quick to mention the shortcomings of other Americans, but said nothing about our own."

Is it indifference or the want of an inquiring mind?

I want to be able to do anything with words: handle slashing, flaming descriptions like Wells, use the paradox with the clarity of Samuel Butler, the breadth of Bernard Shaw and the wit of Oscar Wilde

Scot Fitzgerald

The servant class in Sri Lanka

Maid, Daily Woman, Domestic Help - that's how they are called in most countries. In Sri Lanka they are called just plain "servants." Not just the affluent homes, all homes, labor being available at dime a dozen, employed servants and the shameful conditions under which they toiled for food and a floor to sleep on to which crime this writer is abashed to confess was an accessory and culpable trembles at the thought of what awaits him in Hades, deserves to be told. Perhaps another day.

Meanwhile I relate this episode to which I bear personal testimony. It should give the reader some idea of the treatment of servants I have described.

There was this friend of mine (let's call him Dee Em.) He completed his university degree with high honors in Economics and was planning to do accountancy. In the meantime he wanted to experience firsthand the conditions under which servants toiled in an upscale home. Dressed in soiled clothes he went from house to house offering his services until one young couple agreed to hire him. He of course made it known to them he did not understand English and spoke only Sinhalese.

He worked for one week and without notice walked out on them leaving all his miserable belongings behind. He just could not take it anymore.

He had to be up five O'clock in the morning before the master and lady and went to bed around eleven O'clock long after master and lady had retired. He was given a mat to sleep on the floor in the kitchen and ate left over food. For one week he did not know what was going on in the world as he did not listen to the radio (no television at this time) and was wary about reading the newspapers lying about the house for fear of being caught out. He heard the master and lady speak about him without reservation carelessly in English confident he could not understand the language. Most of the time about making certain everything is kept under lock and key at all times. "Unknown man in the house. Be very careful" husband and wife reminded each other.

Months after he had surreptitiously left their services my friend ran into master and lady in a popular restaurant. He walked over to them and revealed his identity to the amazement and chagrin of master and lady.

The last thing I heard about Dee Em was having qualified as a chartered account he then became a Roman Catholic padre and was employed in the Vatican.

("Injustice is easy not to notice when it affects people different from ourselves, that helps explain the obliviousness of our own generation to inequity today." Nicholas Kristoff in The New York Times praising the book "Just Mercy" by Bryan Stevenson

And Lady Gaga at the 2015 Oscar Awards exposed the collective insensitivity of the American public towards rape in her virtuosic rendition of "Till it happens to you, you won't know."

(The much loved Pope Francis's hands aren't clean either. How is it he is able to continue to look the other way, countenance, nay give his blessings to the principle of "Men Only Women Need not Apply" priesthood? Recently he reiterated women will never be admitted to the priesthood.)

A dose of poison can do its work only once, but a bad book can go on poisoning people's minds for any length of time."

John Murray

CROSS COUNTRY IN A COROLLA

Here I was seated in the drawing room of our first home in the United States on 33 Kings Highway in Shelton, Connecticut (the eagle after flying over oceans and across continents landed in Shelton on August 1, 1985 our son's tenth birth day) a three bed room raised ranch, two car garage, finished basement, perched nay lounging on an elevation, pleasing view in summer and fall perilous in snow and ice, having burnt the bridges, boats and all behind me tenaciously holding on to a work permit with an expiration date, a wife with enormous earning potential that could not be mined for want of proper papers, primary and secondary mortgages on the house, two car loans, start-up expenses of a newly minted settler snowballing and the son in midstream at college.

Why is it I wondered my wants always tend to exceed my wallet.

Our daughter had qualified as an electrical engineer from Clarkson University in Potsdam, New York, and after a transitory dummy run at the Vermont Yankee Nuclear Power Plant was now bubbly, bouncy and in fine fettle to proceed for the Masters at Berkley U.

(Parents get euphoric and are lost in the twilight zone of their children's academic attainments.)

I remember it so well like yesterday's bad salami when the family got into a huddle to determine how best to take our daughter's Corolla to California. It would have been less expensive, less stressful and less *fun* if our daughter flew and the car "shipped out." Alternatively throwing caution to the winds as this family had undeviatingly done always in the past, make a run at the emprise of motoring from Shelton in Connecticut to Berkley in California. To motor or not was the question. A pregnant pause! Three *Ayes and* One *Undecided.* The Ayes thankfully carried the day.

(*Back in our native home on a journey such as this fraught with unknowables Hindus with a view to propitiating the gods break at a temple, ideally of Lord Ganesh, split a coconut at the entrance and proceed. In the absence of a Hindu temple in the locality and no coconut within arm's reach my wife must have done extra time beseeching the gods for a safe journey.)*

It happened many years ago, the time when President Reagan was being pilloried by a democratic congress for illegal sale of weapons to Nicaragua and his one line response "I do not remember" became the boiler plate reply for those who had plenty to hide. So long ago when cell phones were not known, so long ago it is now a fireside story for our grand- children, that I can truthfully say "this much alone I remember." Since all this happened the memory lane through the mists of time has taken too many twists and turns that now I have difficulty negotiating my way.

When traveling the family modus operandi has always been "leave early and arrive safe." And so I recall father, mother and daughter aboard the Corolla, in the gray of dawn we were down route 8 in Shelton not quite ten minutes from home when mighty Indra the Hindu goddess of rain and thunderstorm turned mutinous. She came down fast and furious in thunderous sheets. First independently, then collectively the three of us wondered whether we should turn back. It was unanimous, as we have hitherto done in such situations, that we must like Capt. Ahab in pursuit of the white whale plow on undeterred by the rumblings in high heavens and undistracted from our mission making Indra a little peevish perhaps but mighty proud.

And thus dear friends the "Family Odyssey of Four" fortified by a liberal supply of auto air fresheners and deodorants sans telephone and television (to the delight of mom) we set off on a whim and a prayer not with four but three as our son had taken off to Cleveland to be with his college sweetheart now his wife and will team up later in Columbus, Ohio.

(Cell phones there were none but a monstrosity of a contraption called a "car-'phone" cost circa $3,000.00.)

As the minutes and miles ticked away a pattern emerged. Mom and Dad would occupy the front seats when either was driving while daughter and son loosened up in the rear and then, the order would be reversed.

Driving along the high way while the juniors were asleep my wife and I should we spot a mall without so much as a hush exit and make our way to it much to their annoyance. This way stretching our knees and joints we recharged ourselves for the long road ahead.

(On arrival at the mall for a few minutes our son would be missing. When asked he would say he had to make a telephone call but to this day we do not know who was at the other end.)

With the flow of time memory is getting misty and many incidents which at that time when it happened may have had meaning and poignancy sadly have gone out of my mind's reach. Three incidents however I have managed to retrieve from memory recycle bin put out for removal and would soon have joined the rest in the dump of no return.

(1) The three passengers, mom at my side, daughter and son in the rear were dozing and I at the wheel. The Corolla was heading towards the copper color Utah Mountains nice and dandy on a bright sunny day and asudden I found the car betwixt mountains on a very steep road heading up. The old faithful began coughing and I feared she would soon be out of breath, curl up and go to sleep. There were

no cars ahead and none in the rear view mirror. The three silent passengers were deep into the Land of Nod. I feared if I removed my foot off the pedal the car will slide down. Instinctively without any thought or plan, through sheer power and force of habit (what else could have I done?) I pressed the pedal with all my might down to the metal, to the limit, and the car continued its crawl onwards and up and finally drawing on all its reserve proving its mettle, went over the hump and on to level road. Kudos to Corolla. As for the drama that was unfolding the three passengers were none the wiser, very likely to this day.

(2) As must be expected we had to very often pull over to tank up the car and loosen our limbs. I noticed we were running low on gas and eased to a stop at a primitive looking gas station equipped with very old fashioned pumps. Reminded me of the old west in cowboy movies. Parched land with no vegetation to be seen. I had not the faintest idea where on god's earth this place was. Without actually being able to place your finger on the reason one can always sense when you are not wanted in a place. Vibrations that cannot be seen but can be felt. I observed a couple of stragglers staring at us from inside and outside the station. They must have guessed we were not only from out of state, from out of the United States as well. As I went in to pay for the gas I noticed one uncouth individual walking round the car and examining the Connecticut license plates. Time to vamoose I thought. I was anxious to know what this town was which did not appear keen to have us. Within minutes of taking off on the way the mystery was solved. I should have known. It had to be. It was the "papers please" Sheriff Joe Apaiyo country, the town of Phoenix in Arizona.

Author Jumpha Lahiri described my state of mind accurately. She said, "*Being a foreigner is a sort of lifelong pregnancy – a perpetual wait, a constant burden, a continuous feeling of out of sorts."*

(3) My wife and I consider ourselves very fortunate for there will, for the two of us, never be a redo of this experience. I am referring to the legendary Highway 101 which has inspired many rock bands to sing its praise.

It's the Salome of highways – enticing, demands your full attention and can turn treacherous if you trifle with it. With the vast Pacific Ocean on the left, the tall mountain range on the right on this narrow two way strip with no sidewalks you cannot lose your head. Salome must foremost and forever be in your mind.

The reader must be informed that the four of us on this then hazardous, now looking back exhilarating run are new arrivals having lived in one main road countries. The Galle Road in Sri Lanka, Pademba Road in Freetown, Sierra Leone and Broad Street in Monrovia, Liberia and since expatriate employees are often provided with car and chauffer driving is limited to weekend visits to friends living within shouting distance.

As "luck" would have it mom was in the saddle. The old faithful was inching forward at centipede speed and cars like caravans in the wild-west were trailing behind with angst or amusement we know not. Thus ceremoniously we crawled on all fours down the legendary 101 unable to change riders in mid-gallop until mom to everyone's (phew) relief espied an opening to pull over and our daughter took over the reins.

After a memorable, one time odyssey by a family of four from Connecticut to California in a Corolla sans a cell phone spanning fourteen days motoring across fourteen states with fourteen stop overs we arrived in Haywood San Francisco at the home of our friends the Ratnesars on August 13, 1993.

(*When our daughter was leaving Connecticut for California our neighbors remarked "She's never coming back." Never a truer word spoken; No longer bothered by high electricity bills and heavy underwear, snow, sleet and skidding she's home in the citadel of American Liberalism where black, white, yellow or brown, straight, gay or trans, bisexual or bi- curious this city which author O. Henry described as the "City of the Golden Gate, Bagdad of the New World" is chummy to all.*)

What the family of four remember to this day after all that water had gone under "Chris Christie's bridge" in New Jersey is the warmth with which we were received and the lavish manner we were entertained by our friends at the many stop overs - in Columbus - Ohio, in Chicago - Illinois, in Excalibur - Las Vegas, in Alifant Place - San Diego, in Cardigan Place – Los Angeles and in Haywood Place – San Francisco. To them all, we say a thunderous "*Grazie mille*".

A FAMILY ODYSSEY OF FOUR – *Dad – Mom – Daughter - Son*

From Connecticut to California in a Corolla sans cell phone

Destination – University of California, Berkley

Four Thousand Three Hundred Miles through Fourteen States- in Fourteen Days with stop overs in:

Columbus - Ohio

Chicago – Illinois

Grand Island – Nebraska

Mile High - Colorado

Grand Junction – Colorado

Excalibur - Las Vegas

Alifant Place – San Diego

Cardigan Place – Los Angeles

Haywood – San Francisco

States Covered:

Connecticut – New York – New Jersey – Pennsylvania – Ohio – Illinois – Indiana – Iowa – Nebraska-

Colorado – Utah – Arizona – Nevada - California

Individual miles driven:

Daughter Gaitri – 1900

Son Girisha – 1061

Dad – 738

Mom - 601

Nothing has really happened until it has been recorded.

Virginia Woolf

ESCAPED BY A WHISKER

It was in the early nineteen sixties. I was Secretary to the Board/ Chief Accountant of a prominent Scottish owned hardware and holding company in Colombo, Ceylon, renowned for its quality products and on time delivery. The pay was excellent and the fringe benefits the envy of aspiring accountants. It was an eight- to – four thirty job with an hour for lunch and five day week. If you are working late it means you have been idling during working hours. Bills for goods and services go out on the first working day of each month. Handsome bonus paid twice a year without a miss. You can bank on it. Could a young bachelor ask for more?

Each morning Grigoris would bring the mail over from the post office. Under the supervision of an accountant the mail is sorted by three clerks in a separate room we used to call "mail room." Thereafter the mail is distributed to the heads of departments. Seated in my office I can see Grigoris five feet two or thereabouts bringing the mail bag slung over his right shoulder and the three designated clerks leave their seats and walk towards the mailroom.

Mails for me would be placed in my in tray. I would casually thumb through them and pick out those that called for immediate attention and the rest I would send to the "filing room" marking the dates on which to be brought up for my attention for e.g. 16/1, 14/2/ and so on.

On this day as was the practice the peon placed my mail in the "in tray" and I, leaning forward picked them up with a casualness that comes from one day not being different from any other. Sacre Dieu!

There was a letter from the Inland Revenue Service. Any time you get a letter from Inland Revenue you have reason to be worried. It has something sinister to say. This one looked particularly ominous. Sensing its importance the envelope had not been opened by the clerk. Nervously I slit opened the envelope and read the notice in bold red.

It went something like this. "You are hereby required to pay forthwith a penalty of Rupees 250,000 for nonpayment of income tax." It worked out to be Twenty Five percent on the full amount of one million rupees due.

Sacrebleu! Je suis fini! What do I do now? My goose has been cooked. Here I am working for a company that is brutally unforgiving of incompetence. Sri Lanka at best is the size of West Virginia and well-paying jobs with a foreign firm were thin on the ground. In a matter of days I am going to be checking the wanted ads in the newspapers. That's for sure. Envision a drowning man reaching for a straw or any other.

This is what happened. In the weeks prior when the tax notice was received instead of dunning it for 1/1 (first of January) so that I could pay it well before the due date of 1/15 (January 15) I had dunned it for 1/2 (first of February)

As in life in every work place there is a fixer. Let's say his name was Sandy. Sandy was very adept at fixing. Sandy was the Managing Director's personal consigliore on all matters personnel. *He once said to me Chandra," if you can do these three things you will be a happy man. "What are they?" I asked him. And he replied "Eat Well, Sleep Well, Shit Well"*

With the red notice I go to Sandy's office. All Sandy asks of you is show of respect and this I would give it to him copiously, in spades. He reads the notice and from his countenance I realize he feels he has met his Waterloo. I make it abundantly clear to him I am drowning and he is the straw I am reaching out for. Sandy says "I cannot promise but I'll see what I can do." If you want anything conveyed to the Managing Director tell it to Sandy. From my office I can see Sandy walking into the Managing Director's office. The dots have been collected and joined.

I have worked in eleven companies in four countries in three continents. Of all the bosses I have worked for I have admired this managing director most of all. With a Hobbesian grip on the company he administered with a firm and fair hand. A veteran from the Second World War, a Scotsman, he ran the company like a platoon. "Yes sir", "No sir" "You have your orders." Dismissed" Micro manager par excellence, first man at work and last to depart. Under his stewardship the company thrived from one year to the next, the staff felt their jobs were secure and their monthly paychecks and biannual bonuses never threatened. His instructions were precise in brief typed notes.

(*There were* no *E- mails during this time.)*

Rifled through staff desks and left notes. The only time he took time off from smoking was to light up one more. Believed in one to one dialogue with his executive staff. Did not give a damn for staff meetings or consensus. You have your orders buddy you click your boots and march lock-step if you know what's good for you.

The place ticked like a Swiss watch and always on time. The company paid dividends twice a year to its stockholders and two generous bonuses a year to the entire staff, clerical and executive. You could borrow in advance banking on it. The managing director placed a very high premium on loyalty and integrity. He paid the staff ten percent over the going rate. This way he ensured loyalty and continuity.

As secretary to the board of directors and chief accountant I had life insurance, all medical expenses reimbursed in full and a hefty "401 K" or the equivalent thereof.

I was aware you cannot fight City Hall. The only other thing for me to do is to convey this calamity to the auditors with whom I had very cordial relationship. It was they who recommended me for this job. There is nothing the auditors could do other than listen to my sad story and feel sorry for me.

The company I knew would be giving me the "walking papers." The managing director did not call me up. He would walk past me without as much as a word. I was waiting for the axe to fall.

This state of affairs lasted perhaps a week.

On Saturday afternoon of the same week I was awoken from my nap and was told that a certain gentleman wishes to see me and it's urgent. I shed my sarong, changed and walked up to the front portion of the house. And there was Sandy.

"Chandra! Let's go for a walk." he says. And we began walking towards the beach. He was at a party he says the previous night and he happened to relate the dire situation I was in and that it had been decided by management that I can no longer hold the job. Put bluntly I was going to be fired or as they politely put it "let go." Those present at the party he said were very sympathetic but there was nothing they could do to help. One gentleman present whom Sandy did not know took him to a side and disclosed he was an assessor in the Inland Revenue Office and that he was in charge of my company file. He listened to Sandy patiently and made a suggestion.

Tell the chief accountant (that is me) to write a letter to Inland Revenue requesting additional time to pay the taxes for whatever reason. ***Make certain he advised that the date on the letter is prior to the date the tax was due. The letter must be sent by ordinary mail.***

On Sunday night I went over to Sandy's drafted a letter requesting little extra time to pay the tax as we were currently reorganizing our finances predated it and mailed it by ordinary mail on Monday morning. I am somewhat fuzzy here but this is the gist. I informed mail room that any letter from Inland Revenue should be brought to me post – haste.

I felt I should keep the auditors appraised. One partner listened to all I said and remarked "I did not hear anything you said. Desperate problems call for desperate remedies." Even today those words are ringing in my ears. Just as Guy Fawkes once said, "A desperate disease requires a dangerous remedy."

And I waited what seemed ages piled upon ages and the waiting was lacerating. I felt like an ant running on a hot frying pan. One nervous week went by, two weeks went by. Like a crouching beast in the jungle destined to slay or be slain by the events to follow I nervously bided my time. And then the Inland Revenue letter arrived. The letter referred to my request for time and that I should appear for an interview with the assessor – the same assessor whom Sandy had met at the party.

Sandy and I called on the assessor by appointment. Dead pan and poker faced without interruption he heard my convoluted story. I produced proof that the company had absolutely no liquidity problem and that we were merely awaiting his response to our request for additional time.

I remember this very well. I was facing the window and the strong tropical sunlight was getting into my eyes causing tears. He said we could ignore the penalty and pay the tax only. When I returned to my office I paid the tax as originally called. There was no official letter waiving the penalty. My guess is the file was closed as we heard no more.

When Sandy met the assessor on another occasion informally he had commented that he felt sorry for me when he saw me in tears.

The Managing Director never discussed this episode with me. Sandy the Fixer Generalissimo would have filled him in laced with heavy layers of embellishment and drama as he is known to do.

Every nightmare ends in daylight.

I have a rather plain and direct prose style. For me the words must be like a pane glass that you look through, not at.

Ken Follet

THIS IS NO FICTION

I was reading Tijan M. Sallah's story "Innocent Terror" from the collection "Under African Skies" in which an innocent cook is murdered by a Lebanese and he walks scot-free. The following exchange hit me hard. I have lived in Sierra Leone and Liberia for approximately fifteen years and everything stated here is true.

"The catalogue of Lebanese misbehavior was lengthy – from receiving most favored treatment from the banks and from all respectable government institutions to the rude flouting of local customs to sometimes engaging in incest and drugs…"

"These Lebanese," remarked Badou, the younger Tambedou, "they think they own Africa. *I heard that in Sierra Leone they run the state."*

"I am not surprised," commented a friend.

I even heard one of them …a powerful one … in Sierra Leone, who had his private plane, private bank."

To this I can attest. I was there and saw it all. I even know the gentleman they are referring to. As Chief Accountant of a large government corporation and later as Accountant General in Sierra Leone I had to, not by choice but by necessity interact with these Lebanese. I have spoken on several occasions to the gentleman who had a private bank, private plane and more. In Liberia I worked for one of these very powerful Lebanese. Labor laws did not apply. The staff had to work until they were dismissed for the "day" which "day" begins at eight in the morning and often went on till eleven in the night with a half hour break for lunch, six days a week, sometimes Sundays too.

According to the terms of my employment, in one case, I was to be provided with a car. It was root canal without morphine to eventually get one, a badly used car which leaked petrol.

On the day I landed in Liberia I was met at the airport and the gentleman who received me took away my passport ostensibly to clear me through customs and immigration and thereafter I did not see my passport. This way they kept you in check. There was no one you can complain to. All government officials were on their "pay roll." Some of the Lebanese businessmen had a direct line to the president. Laws did not apply to them. The natives were in constant fear of these Lebanese businessmen. They lumped whatever insults were dished out to them. They had nowhere to go for recourse.

I was Chief Accountant and the work was a wholesale nightmare. The owner a Lebanese gentleman would come around ten in the morning and take away all the previous day's takings leaving only the checks to be deposited. A great deal of guess work, fabrication and juggling of numbers went into the preparation of accounts for audit and the audit was nothing short of a sham.

I bid adieu to this company and joined a locally owned private company and when the the coup d' tat by the army that resulted in the assassination of the president and the public hanging of several prominent cabinet members occurred with my family I fled the country.

A good reader is one who has imagination, memory, a dictionary, and some artistic sense.

Nabakov

THE HOUSE OUR FATHER BUILT.

Wilbur Wright, one of the Wright Brothers, the other being Orville, the inventors of the first viable airplane who taught the world how to fly gives us this advice:

"If I were giving a young man advice as to how he might succeed in life, I would say to him, pick out a good father and mother."

My memory is fragmentary and getting fainter with years. It's therefore paramount I record what I can recollect before they, moving beyond the rim of recall become irretrievable and lost forever.

As mentioned in my book "Mining My Own Life" my father while living in Ratnakara Place in Sri Lanka on his return from Malaysia planned to build a house in the greater Colombo area and with my mother make a home for the rest of his retirement years. But Moira had other plans.

The communal riots of May 1958 drove him to cut and run to the north, to Sandilipay to the village of his parents and grandparents, to the faith and flesh of his forefathers.

He had some well- earned savings socked away and a plot of bare land in the neighboring village of Chankanai given to my mother as dowry. How does one set up home on bare land? It had to be built on. His brothers and sister realizing he was in a quandary magnanimously offered to share their home until the new house was built.

My parents who have always been fiercely independent and valued their private space turned down the big hearted offer of temporary shelter by the siblings opted to live for a time in sub Appalachian "comfort." He rented a shack sans running water, sans indoor toilet, sans bathtub, shower or electricity, crumbling side walls, cracked ceiling overhead, cavernous floor underfoot over which you must tip-toe but thanks to the crystalline clear though slightly brackish well water and save a couple of tumbled down odd pieces of furniture - a couple of chairs and a sofa nothing else to boast about.

At this time I was serving articles with a firm of Chartered Accountants in Colombo and during holidays I would visit my parents and live with them in this you may call it a "house." After dark my mother would light up a couple of oil lamps which I would carry from room to room mindful of moths and lizards and cockroaches and other creeping, crawling creatures. I bathed at the well and relieved at the outhouse. The house was situated in the middle of a large compound of fruit trees of many kinds. During the day I would lie on the sofa in the tropical sun, soak up the gentle, friendly breeze and read until dark. Very early morning my father would be up and about preparing to leave for the site where the new house was being built. It was within hailing distance. For a man who had won prizes in walking competitions (fifty miles and over) this must have been a walk in the park. A breeze!

My mother would prepare his lunch and armed with this he would set out for the work site where he will stay until dark making certain the workers were doing their part.

I have no idea how much the house cost and how he financed it. Once and only once he asked me how Brown & Co shares were selling. I checked it up and informed him. From this I gathered he had his savings in company shares.

When I consider that my father who went to Malaysia wholly under British Raj in search of employment with nothing more than a high school diploma and retired as chief clerk in the Malayan

Railways having to get by on a fixed salary with a spouse a home maker and two boys to boot now managing on a flat monthly pension by far princely it must have given my parents monumental satisfaction to move into the new house.

The house was named "Yogamaligai" – a composite of Yoga being part of my mother's name and Maligai in Tamil means mansion. It was more than a house. It was our home.

I liked this house immensely. I felt relaxed and at home under its roof. Allow me to quote from "Sathyavan and Savithri" a true story I wrote in my blog many years ago.

"Seated in the open veranda of my parent's home in Chankanai in arid Jaffna province north of Ceylon, from where I could see the sub post office, within walking distance of the only bicycle repair shop, the fish market, church, a temple, the zinc roofed cinema hall where shows are cancelled when it rains, far, far from the madding crowd of Colombo, I see boys after school jauntily in a pack, following girls on their way home."

Yes reader. It was nice. It was homey. This is how a fish must feel when it is thrown back into the sea or a caged bird when set free. My father having watered the garden which he alone must do, my offer to help rebuffed, would be seated in the far end of the veranda and smoke his cheroot and my mother thrilled to the core, now on high that I am home would excitedly be walking to and fro without a single purpose having informed neighbors long before the exact date of my arrival.

My parents wanted a house with three bed rooms to be certain in the event my brother and I should visit at the same time (seldom happened) we could all be comfortable.

At this point the words of E.M.Forster comes to mind

("A wonderful physical tie binds the parents to the children, and by some strange irony it does not bind us children to our parents. For if it did, if we could answer their love not with gratitude but with equal love, life would lose much of its pathos and much of its squalor and we might be wonderfully happy.")

The last time I saw this house was in 1982 when I was employed briefly in Colombo, Sri Lanka. Since then my parents have passed away. The fighting between the Sinhalese and Tamils which had its genesis in May of 1958 intensified and metastasized like stage four cancer, nay like paralysis to my village. The army got suzerainty over the land of my forefathers and behaved the way all occupying forces do – rape, arson and loot boldly openly in broad daylight.

(The intrusion of the army, the strong-arm agents of the central government, making unwelcome incursions into the land and lives of the Jaffna Tamils transfigured the northern part of the country to an extent that it no longer retains the bucolic charm and primal innocence of yester years.)

As recent as in March 2016 I asked my brother what came of the house our father built. This was his reply.

"The army ran over Jaffna and *Yogamaligai* was occupied by the army. When the army left, the house was left wide open and most things were looted. Later our neighbor J's son occupied the house and lived there without our permission."

My friend John related this to me while we lived in Freetown, Sierra Leone. His father had put all his savings into a house built under his supervision in a place called Kotahena in the suburb of Colombo, Sri Lanka. John said to me not a single crack in the wall or scratch on the furniture would go unattended pronto. The house was his joy. He was proud he had something to show his children and grandchildren for the years of toil in the office. During the communal riots of 1958 thugs looted all his belongings and set fire to the house burning it down to ashes right in his presence.

The gods have been kind and for this I genuflect in gratitude. The blood thirsty hounds of karma did not pursue my parents to the biting end. My parents went to their last resting place innocent of what came of the **"House our father built."**

Poet Robert Frost wrote that home is the place where, when you have to go there they have to take you in. The prodigal son after philandering his youth and squandering his wealth was able to return to the embrace of his father because there was a physical house to go to. One can make a home out of a house however humbly appointed it may be but without a house of brick and cement you have only your memories to live with.

Suggested reading:

Thomas Wolfe - "You Cannot Go Home Again"

Sidney Poitier – "The Measure of a Man" wherein he states – "After eight years of struggle I was able to return to my father's house, but in certain ways I was never able to go back home"

As for me home will soon cease to exist even in the mothballs of my memory. Author Jumpha Lahiri cuts through the saccharine sentimentality and lip reverence to patriotism and forces us to look at the land of our choice the right way, the sane- way.

This is what Jumpha Lahiri has to say:

"A place to which you feel the strongest attachment isn't necessarily the country you are tied to by blood or birth. It's the place that allows you to become yourself. … And as a first generation American I can truly say that America happens to be the place that allows me to become myself. For that I am eternally grateful."

Pulitzer Prize winner Jumpha Lahiri of Bengali (Indian) extract was born in London, raised in Rhode Island, U.S.A. presently lives in Brooklyn, U.S.A.

If I may add another hue to this rainbow – Home to me is not the country where I was born. No sir!

Home is where I feel at home.

Any country wherein conditions are conducive, ripe and ideal for the exercising your god given potential to the fullest, that surely must be the country you should swear fealty to.

If you are going to be a writer there is nothing I can say to stop you;
if you are not going to be a writer nothing I can say will help you

James Baldwin

HOT AND SPICY CHICKEN CURRY

Author Joyce Carol Oates as a little girl used to cart around a fowl given to her which she adored. One day the favored chicken was gone. When I read this my own experience came to mind.

My parents while I was a brat and living in Malaysia gave me a tiny, pretty new born chick and was told I should look after it. Every day when I returned from school I would feed him and saw him grow into a full- fledged fowl. During weekends he was my constant companion. I gave him a name which I do not remember now.

One day when I came home from school he was nowhere to be seen. Like Joyce Carol Oates I looked for him everywhere. The usual places. Called out his name with a fistful of rice and normally he would have come running to me. Not today. Finally distraught and heartbroken I asked my mother where he was and the reply I got was "why don't you come and have your lunch now. We can look for him later."

I obeyed. *Enjoyed a good hot and spicy chicken curry and went out to play with my neighbors.*

Language reveals the man. Speak that I may see.

Ben Johnson

GOSPEL TRUTH OR IS IT "LOST IN TRANSLATION?"

We are given to understand God charged Moses to write down his utterances - "Write down these words" he commanded "for in accordance with these, I have made a covenant with you and Israel." And Moses dutifully wrote it down in his native diction Hebrew with a generous sprinkling of Aramaic. In brief this constituted the *Old Testament.*

The *New Testament* comprises of several books, of Mark, Mathew, Luke and John. They were written in Greek the lingua Franca of the time.

The *Quran*, the Muslims claim was verbally revealed by God to Muhammad through the angel, Gabriel (Jibril) at a leisurely swagger of twenty three years. These Holy revelations were written down by several scribes who were companions of Muhammad. It was written in Arabic.

The *Bhagavad Gita,* Gospel of the Hindus is the sermon delivered by the charioteer Lord Krishna to the warrior Arujna in the battle field of Kurukshektra amidst the cacophonous din of conch shells and the swish of arrows in the epic battle between the cousins, the Pandavars and the Kauravas which lasted eighteen days.

We are told the whole event was known to the sage Vyasa who narrated it to Lord Ganesha who then wrote it down in Sanskrit.

How much were the scribes who had the onerous responsibility of recording for posterity able to remember? How much did they imagine? How much inconvenient truth did they excise? And how much that were laudable did they embellish?

God alone knows!

What we are reading today are translations from Hebrew and Greek and Arabic and Sanskrit to English, medieval to modern, an inebriating holy cock tail of fact and fiction.

If you doubt me here's what Thomas Mallon has to say in "Stolen Words", "The Classic Book On Plagiarism" - "The Romans rewrote the Greeks. Virgil is, in a broadly imitative way, Homer, **and for that matter, typologists can find most of the Old Testament in the New.** The medieval monks rewrote, quite literally, such manuscripts as they could find."

Were the Scribes up to the Same Mischief?

I had just arrived from Malaysia, in the early dawn of my teens and was admitted to Jaffna College (here college is high school.) It was end of year and it was customary for every class to have a party and the class teacher who will be leaving is the chief guest. An "address paper" is presented. It works like this. On a colorful paper with a beautiful border nice things are written by an outsider about the departing teacher. One from the class is selected to copy it and read it at the party to which other teachers too are invited.

My class mates claiming I was adept at calligraphy wanted me to do the honors to write and read the "address paper" and I agreed.

When transcribing I observed one line went like this. Mr. C.S.P. is "a true Christian gentleman" blah- blah.

I was troubled. I could understand what it is to be a gentleman, may be a "true gentleman" but a "true *Christian* gentleman" I did not understand. I suspected it was a mischievous ploy to separate the Christians from the "heathens" the unbelievers and so on. It did not pass the sniff test and so I left the word Christian out and wrote "Mr. C.S.P. is a true gentleman" and so forth.

While reading I felt uneasy when I came to this portion but batted on regardless with a wink and a nod to my conscience. I do not know whether it was noticed. No one commented on my editing.

Looking back with retirement wisdom I now realize how petty and puerile my action had been.

And very likely the scribes too being human with selective memory and an axe to grind may have been up to this kind of mischief. Embellish the virtues, excise the vice.

My writing is all mixed up. I'm jumping from one thing to another and sometimes I seriously wonder whether anyone will ever be interested in this novel. They'll probably call it "the musings of an ugly duckling"

Ann Frank – "The Diary of Ann Frank"

What a fine country America must be to live in I would say to myself.

During my residence (residence I call it because I lived a nomadic existence) in Malaysia, Ceylon, Sierra Leone, Liberia, I used to tell myself "Oh these lucky blokes who live in the United States."

In my book "Mining My Own Life" I did mention that for a period when I was studying accountancy I lived in the home of my friend's uncle and aunt whose daughter won an American Field Service scholarship and spent a few months in Pennsylvania, U.S.A. On her return she was all gung ho about the U.S. A. I was carried away with everything she had to say. It was even better than what Dick Wittington thought about London. Among her narrative one stood out. Children going to school were bused. All they had to do was stand out of the house and the bus will take them to their school. Isn't that nice I would think to myself.

And then I see this.

While I was working as controller at the City Plumbing and Construction Company in Monrovia, Liberia one morning as I was parking my car two buses speed up, screech to a halt and park. Very close to my office there were the American school for American children and another for the British. I saw American soldiers hurriedly go into the school for American children get all the children out, shoved them into the bus and speed away. Strange I thought and went about my work. The next morning there was a coup d' etat staged by the body guard Samuel K. Doe and President Tolbert was assassinated. Ministers of government were swinging from ropes in a public square. While we were huddled in abject fear in a friend's home the Americans were given protection.

We read to know that we are not alone

C.S. Lewis

WHAT WOULD YOU CALL IT?

Is it Serendipity?

(*The making of happy and unexpected discovery by accident*)

Is it Karma?

(*The spiritual principle of cause and effect- the actions of an individual in the present life influence the future life of that individual*)

Is it Fortuity?

(*A Macabre or genial coincidence,* no more)

Is it Maktub? (It's written)

The Hindu Tamils have a word for it – Thalai Eluthu

Is it Historical Determinism?

Events are historically predetermined. There is a belief that historical and by logical extension present and future events unfold according to predetermined sequences. Determined by whom we wonder? Did not Anton Chekov in "Attack on nerves" say "Against my will *an unknown force* has led me to these mournful shores?"

Was it just inevitableness that the Protestant Reformation occurred when it did; the American Revolution occurred when it did and the slow and steady evolution of parliamentary system of government as we see it in the United Kingdom?

Is this all just a cosmic fluke?

In explaining their destiny Frederick Douglas and Abraham Lincoln quoted the same line from Shakespeare in "Hamlet"

"There is a destiny that shapes our ends

Rough-hew them how we will" Hamlet to Horatio Act 5 Scene 2

In Mathew 10:29-31 we are informed "Are not two sparrows sold for a penny? Yet not one of them will fall to the ground outside your father's care."

Into which of the above classification does the discovery of Moses in a basket made of bulrushes along the bank of the Nile fall into?

Every one of us has at some time benefited from bonanzas like manna from heaven consequentially metamorphic just when we needed it most.

Here I recount my experience.

(1)

Those who have thumbed through my book "Mining My Own Life" must know of my tortuous journey to obtaining a permit (casually referred to as "work permit" which alone allows you to work in the United States. The work permit only allows you to work in the country, no more. The entre to citizenship is a Green Card (by far green in color – perhaps alludes to green light to citizenship.)

My attorney was a kind man. Unlike Bill Clinton's spurious claim Cohen really felt my pain. I had worked in the U.S. for five years and had reached the end of the trail of extensions to my work permit. I had held responsible positions in accounting in Sri Lanka, Sierra Leone (as Accountant General) and Liberia but my professional qualifications were home grown (Sri Lanka) and my accounting experiences mostly foreign. I had to now satisfy the immigration authorities that I have the professional qualifications and experience that is exceptional that will merit consideration for a green card. My attorney forwarded my resume to professional evaluators for their opinion for submission to Immigration. These professionals unfamiliar with foreign qualifications, their evaluations were tepid at best. My attorney knew through experience these evaluations are bound to fall short of Immigrations' high threshold. Time was running out. I could sense the window closing. In seven to ten days Immigration would mark *finis* on my file and I would have to sell the house and cars, Bric- a- brac–and all and with wife and two children say adios to "the land of the free and the home of the brave" and gypsy to another country. For me it was the last helicopter leaving Saigon and I must get on board. You could hear the death rattle. Yeah! I have not forgotten these days.

Cohen decided to make a last ditch effort and give it a final do or die shot. There was in Seattle, Washington a very respectable professional whose evaluations carried weight with Immigration. His specialty was evaluating foreign qualifications. He decided to call him. It was *Friday* around four thirty in the evening. He kept the phone ringing for a while until he heard a voice at the other end. The gentleman (let's call him Mr. Pro) had locked his office and stepped out. Commencing Monday he was on a three week vacation touring Europe (he does not work on Saturdays we learnt later) and was going to ignore the phone and proceed home. He said to my attorney he had never ever done this before. He opened his office and picked up the phone. My attorney explained my doomsday situation. Mr. Pro said to Cohen "Fax me his resume and I will review it and fax my evaluation over the week-end.

Well! Should I say Saturday and Sunday I was walking on hot coals? The waiting was a Trial by Fire a baptism that would change forever the lives of my family. Big Time!

On Monday around midday I get a call from Cohen. "Chandraraj I have to see you right away." From the timbre of Cohen's mono tone I could never guess whether the news was going to be good or bad. My office was on the corner of Vanderbilt and 44th. I took the # 6 Down Town to China Town, walked up Broadway and into his office. He handed me the evaluation. It was Comme Il Faut; "On the button", "On the nose." Call it anyway you like. Right then and there we completed forms, dots, dashes and all and the rest as we are won't to say is history.

(*At this time there was one of three ways I could claim my green card. With the family travel to Sri Lanka – by virtue of heritage I was now a Sri Lankan national making a total as of today three- Canada, or to the last place of residence – Freetown, Sierra Leone where all the papers were being held. Even though it would cost much much more I preferred Freetown because the papers were there and I had good connections in Freetown.*)

Now for the scary part! Cohen says to me "Chandraraj if for some reason the interview should go sour and you are turned down you can kiss good bye about ever returning to the U.S. I have never given my home telephone number to any of my clients. Here it is call me if you have a problem. I really do not know how I can be of help. Make sure you take all the documents called for." By Gad in the nervous excitement of so much that was expected of me I failed to appreciate and appropriately thank him for his generous offer of help.

Documents called for were many and varied. Copies of one year's bank statements, academic certificates, police clearances from every country I had lived in and on and on. Made three sets of copies. One my wife to carry, I to carry the other and one set left with my brother in law in Connecticut. From the time we left home for Kennedy driven by my brother in law to the moment of the interview it was painful. Suppose the Embassy official should be nasty, picky, for whatever reason, who knows and turns it down then what next? "Our daughter, house, cars are still in the U.S. "Chandraraj makes no difference to the I.N.S" Cohen had "assured" me.

The American embassy in Freetown is located next to the Cotton Tree a very well- known land mark, a large sturdy tree spread out like an umbrella over Freetown, the capital. It is here that slaves from North America were set free hence the name Free Town. We arrive at the office at the appointed time, ten O'clock all sweaty. The embassy official all smiles says "I am sorry you had to come all the way. Unfortunately those are the rules. I see you are from Shelton, Connecticut. My house is along the Housatonic." Our son and he get into a serious back and forth on football. He gives us a document with the official seal on it saying this document entitles you to all the rights and privileges of a United States citizen.

I will be doing injustice to my memory if I fail to quote from Bruce Nordstrom's "Leave it better than you found it." which never fails to give me tremendous joy. Here in Nordstrom's words:

"I am writing this for my grand children to read after I am gone to let them know what the average immigrant has to go through… Not that it was only worse for me than a lot of others but after reading this they should be happy they were born in America."

Broke journey in Amsterdam, visited the art museum along the canal, the head of John the Baptist being offered to Salome on a platter the most impressive of all, did a boat ride on the canal, "turned the car and headed for home."

(2)

Over thirty years ago I was employed at the Treasury in Sierra Leone (West Africa.) It's a tedious and time consuming chore to successfully get a telephone call through to Sierra Leone from Europe or South Asia. During my stay of over ten years I had not made or received a call.

While I was at work at the Treasury much to my surprise I was informed there was a call for me from the United States and I should take the call on the third floor. My wife's brother informed me that my father in law had passed away in Ceylon and he from Connecticut and the sister from London plan to attend the funeral.

My wife and I agreed attending the father's funeral was paramount. There was a snag that had to be overcome. Due to adverse sterling balance of payments Sierra Leone was experiencing at that time the governor of the Central Bank had imposed draconian restrictions on foreign exchange remittances especially for foreign travel. All permits for release of funds had to be approved by the governor and to further compound and complicate the problem I had only recently returned from my contractual overseas vacation.

Girding up the loins of my mind I made my way upstairs to the office of my boss the Financial Secretary. As I peeped into his office I saw him in a *tete a tete* with the governor of the Central Bank. As I turned round to depart I heard my boss call out "Raj you can come in." I let the two who mattered most in this situation, the Financial Secretary and his boss, the Governor know the quandary I was in. Sierra Leoneans I must mention *en passant* turn tenderhearted and magnanimous when dealing with those grieving from the death of a loved one. The governor before I could complete my plea picks up the phone and orders his deputy that funds may be released for my wife's travel.

My wife from Freetown Sierra Leone in West Africa, her brother from Connecticut U.S.A., the sister from London in the United Kingdom meet at Schiphol airport, Amsterdam and together travel to Colombo, Ceylon joining the sister already there to say "*Adieu Appah - Until We Meet Again.*"

(3)

We lived in Monrovia, Liberia for a number of years. Of all the countries I have lived in I feared Monrovia most of all. The cops are menacing and ordinary folks look upon you as a walking, talking A.T.M. Our friend Maha once in his car slowed down at a crossing and was stopped by a cop. "Sir you were thinking of committing a traffic offense" he says and takes out his note book. A few dollars exchanged hands and he was on his way. A foolish Indian teacher tried to be cute. He was determined not to reach for his wallet and was thrown in jail and languished there until the principal of the school bailed him out. Never leave home without your wallet and make sure you have just enough and not too much for it will be emptied. If you don't have money he will say "Take me to your house you must have plenty there." You don't want that.

One night we left our son a baby at that time at a friend's and with our daughter ventured out whistling in the dark. Our destination was about five minutes away. We were stopped by a cop. Reason? Lights were not on. Not true. Our daughter began crying and so the cop softened his tone. He followed us to our friend's at Mamba Point where we paid him off.

You can understand if I say we limit our driving to the absolute minimum. One fine Sunday afternoon we got bold and went on a long drive on a lonely road with barren land on either side. After an hour of driving we turned back. Half an hour in and the car began making weird noises. I cannot change a spare tire for the love of God. That is as far as my knowledge of motor mechanism goes. The first thing an ignoramus does is open the hood and look inside. That's what I did. I did not see anything out of place. Really I did not know what I was looking for. There's no Triple A here and cell phones were not heard of at this time. Just who am I going to call anyway?

Just then we see a pickup approaching us from a distance at break neck speed kicking up a lot of dust.

(Remember Omar Sharif in Lawrence of Arabia on a camel approaching a Bedouin in the desert stealing a sip of water is gunned down)

We really feared for our lives. We do not want any help – just leave us alone was my silent prayer.

The driver and another riding shot gun shot past us and hundred yards away screeched to a halt. They turned round and approached us. When the hood of the car is ajar, two kids and the two adults looking like having just escaped from the lunatic asylum out on the road it does not need a Sigmund Freud to figure out.

I mumbled something. I don't know whether they heard me. One guy took some tools from the pickup and the next thing I know my Peugeot 504 was purring like a friendly Schnauzer. The two of them turned back, walked to the pickup and just as suddenly as they appeared they disappeared into the distant dust.

Most of my research consists of googling in search of factoids that I can distort beyond recognition.

Dave Barry

WOULD SOMEONE EXPLAIN?

Mozart wrote his first symphony when he was eight years old and was playing in public when he was six.

Helen Keller was born dumb deaf and blind but overcame obstacles through dint of perseverance and the angelic help of Anne Sullivan

There are others born with debilitating disabilities not so blessed who go to their graves miserable and abandoned. Parents of these children grieve interminably asking the question "Why me?"

Hitler, Idi Amin, Stalin and Assad among many others were directly and consciously responsible for the annihilation of several thousands of innocent human beings. What came of them?

We tend to explain the mystery mostly by drawing on our spiritual schooling – Christianity, Islam, Buddhism, Hinduism and so on.

I as a Hindu believe in life after life. I do not believe in Serendipity, Fortuity or Lucky Chance. I believe in the Karmic principle of cause and effect. We reap in the next life what we sow in this. As you sow so shall you reap! To me this appears to make sense.

And yet I am dumb enough to feel I may be wrong. Wrong by a lifetime!

President Jimmy Carter a man of immense faith writes in "A full life" Reflections at Ninety:

"Reaching my ninetieth birthday is a good time to look back on moments that changed my life and reflect on some of the memories that are especially important to me. Some of these events affected me profoundly or taught me lessons large and small. Others are amusing and some make me contemplate who I was at that time. There are some that I enjoyed and savor, and others *I wish had never happened or that I could change.*"

Does he not believe in "Opus Dei" (*the work of God*), "Maktub" (*It is written*) "Karma" (*cause and effect*) and there was nothing he could have done to change the events the way it unfolded.

The song by Doris Day which most children know by rote comes to mind. The mother here would love to make the child happy with promises of a grand future but does not. On the contrary she tells the child just the way she has come to understand life – "what will be, will be." "Que Sera, Sera."

So long as one like a babe is suckling at the breasts of Lakshmi or Fortuna (the goddesses of fortune) he does not contemplate on matters such as fate, life here or hereafter. He accepts the munificence of the goddesses as his just desserts. He is a changed man when disaster hits him hard in his solar plexus. He then spirals not into unconsciousness but into a painful realization that there is more to life, something beyond human cognition as we see in the case of Amy Robach, the Good Morning America anchor.

In her book "Better" Amy writes, "I have so many reflections that begin with *what if* and *thank God. What if* I had stayed at my previous job at NBC and never switched to ABC? *Thank God* I jumped networks. *What if* I hadn't become a larger part of the *Good Morning America* family, which happened only because of an unexpected twist in GMA host Robin Robert's second cancer battle? I'd filled in for Robin every other week for nearly a year while she was on leave for a bone marrow transplant to fight myelodysplastic syndrome. *Thank God* I was the one who got to step in. If these things hadn't happened, I might never have received the email that ultimately saved my life.

"I've never been a big believer in *fate*. Too many awful things happen to too many wonderful people for me to accept that **there's a larger plan "for the greater good."** But that said, I have to admit, the events that led to my diagnosis all felt very **fated."**

If I truly believe everything is predetermined you may wish to know why before crossing the road do I look left and right.

I have sought happiness everywhere, but I have found it nowhere except in a little corner with a little book.

Thomas a' Kempis

Where Were You When Time Stood Still

I know where I was.

1. When Gandhi was assassinated – 1/30/1948

In Jaffna, Sri Lanka

I was at Jaffna College (a high school really) in Vaddokoddai a village in the northern part of Ceylon in the Table Tennis room playing Table Tennis when students came rushing in carrying portable radios. I heard Prime Minister Nehru address the nation saying "Bapuji is no more" and the weeping of millions could be heard.

2. When Kennedy was assassinated. – 10/22/1963

In Colombo, Sri Lanka

I dropped in at my Uncle's home in Colombo and found his wife sobbing. When I enquired what happened she said she learnt just now Kennedy had been assassinated.

3. Moon Landing – 7/20/1969

In Colombo, Sri Lanka

From the time I returned from work in the evening I had the radio with me following the commentary. I was determined to stay awake at the time of landing. I got into bed with the radio close to me. I heard the now famous words of Neil Armstrong as it was happening.

"One small step for man, one giant leap for mankind"

(*There was no television at this time in Ceylon*)

4. When the last helicopter took off from the roof of the American Embassy in Saigon bearing the last Americans and a few of the embassy staff – 4/29/1975

In Colombo, Sri Lanka

I was on vacation in Ceylon from Sierra Leone and visiting my uncle in Bambalapitiya (Sri Lanka) Like Jane Fonda and Cassius Clay I too felt the war was an atrocity an indelible scar on the American image.

5. When the Challenger exploded – 1/28/1986

In Westport, Connecticut

I was working in the accounts department at Norden Systems in Westport when all my colleagues dropped whatever they were doing and were heading towards the cafeteria close by. When I joined them I heard over the radio President Reagan's address to the nation.

6. When Nine Eleven occurred- 9/11/2001

In Hamden, Connecticut

My wife and I are experiencing the empty nest syndrome and yet strangely there is always a third person in the house – the television which is turned on all day and most of the night.

I was in the bedroom in our home in Shelton attending to matters nothing momentous and looking up I see a plane go into Twin Towers and there after several replays of it. Just then the telephone rings and it's our daughter – in – law calling from out of state inquiring whether I had seen the horror on television.

7. When the first African- American became president of the United States of America. - 1/20/2009

In Hamden, Connecticut in the U.S.A. (glued to the television all day and the following day) when Barack Obama the first African (Kenya) American (Hawaii) was elected president of the United States of America

(I do not recall the assassination of Martin Luther King Jr on 4/4/1968. I was in Sri Lanka at that time)

How sacred is the written word that paints portraits in our souls.

Jennifer Morton

Queen Scout

We who lived in Colonial times had a secret fascination for all things British. In this mind set to be a Queen Scout to me would have been a proud achievement.

Sir Robert Baden Powell; Sir David Attenborough; Sir Richard Attenborough; David Beckham, Richard Branson all illustrious Queen Scouts. I admired them all.

I would have loved to be a Queen Scout but it was not to be. In such circumstances what then do parents do? They want their children to go where they could not. Parents want to see their children move the ball further down the field. Like a body builder pumping iron heaving under the weight adds another ten pounds to his heavy weight. Like a relay runner pumped out at the end of his lap hands over the baton to the new runner - his child – who is restlessly waiting, in fact beginning his run looking ahead with hand stretched back to get hold of the baton and make a dash for it. And the father looking on hoping the race will be won.

This is not the hallucination of a crank. This is not a yearning for a heavenly pie in the sky. History is suffuse with examples. Suffice it is to cite two.

Sanjay L. Shah remained in the Jomo Kenyatta airport in Nairobi, Kenya for thirteen months until he was granted British citizenship he was entitled to. He wanted his son now in his tweens to receive a British university education. He was a manual worker.

The father of tennis star of international fame Stefan Edberg mortgaged his only house to send his son to be coached in the United Kingdom.

We were living in Freetown, Sierra Leone and into our lives parachutes the man to this day I admire without exception the most – Vincent Spring. A mensch with all the finest attributes this word has come to mean. A British national loaned to the Sierra Leone Treasury where I was Accountant General.

A gentleman to his fingertips he fought in the Second World War and honored by the Queen for his outstanding services, a Masters in accounting and in his mid-sixties was preparing for his doctorate. In him I saw the happy fusion of a scholar's erudition and an artist's imagination. One who was good with his hands and had a sound head on his shoulders. Always eager to be of assistance, he was very kind to his subordinates.

He was a Queen Scout. He had to be. He encouraged our son to become one.

(*My wife and I had the very good fortune of visiting Vincent and Audrey in their home in Devon, England.*)

EAGLE SCOUT

And so when we migrated to the U.S.A. my wife and I encouraged our son to become an Eagle Scout. We followed his progress through every stage to the day of his investiture as an Eagle Scout.

He has joined the exclusive club to which the following preeminent gentlemen belong.

Neil Armstrong

Willie Banks

Thomas Foley

Bill Gates

H. Ross Perot

Donald Rumsfeld

Gerald Ford

A father admonishes his teen age son, "You act as if though you are smarter than me?"

"Of course I am" answers the son.

"How come?" the father questions mildly rankled.

"Because" replies the son bemused, "Your father was a small time farmer but mine is a justice of the Supreme Court."

"..And the fruits will out do what the flowers have promised."

I want to be an honest man and a good writer.

James Baldwin

The Art of Mourning

"Blessed are they that mourn for they shall be comforted." (Mathew 5:4)

"Since every death diminishes us a little we grieve – not so much for the death as for ourselves."

Lynn Caine

To mourn and grieve when a relative or a friend has been bereaved is natural and it's human.

The Malays and Chinese down our road in Sentul, Malaysia would, seated in a tent talk in whispers or refrain from talking totally. They consider the deceased blessed for they are henceforth rid of the heart aches and pains the living must endure. There is a potent prayer in Hinduism - "*pravathiruka varam thara venrum aiyane*" Translated from Tamil it means, "Lord bless that I shall have no more births"

An Irish wake is not known for stodginess or sobriety, anything but somber. In parts of Indonesia it is a raucous affair. In New Orleans true to tradition you will hear jazz funeral music. In Madagascar the family people dance with the bodies and pass family secrets to the deceased to be carried to the next world.

This I have witnessed firsthand and at close quarters the way the Tamil Hindus living in the northern part of Ceylon (now Sri Lanka) conduct themselves in similar circumstances. It is bordering on comic. Say Ponammah down the road has died. The ladies in white saree will visit the home daily to offer their condolences. On the day the cremation is to take place the ladies seated on the floor in a group, hugging the lady on the left and the right will belt out at full throttle. They will after a while take a break and at times indulge in gossip. When a new person walks in she will join the women seated on the floor and a 'big cry" is set off. This goes on until each one remembering what chores at home have still to be done slips out. Ladies who have visited a funeral home will not on their return enter their homes until they have had a bath at the well side. Women do not go to the crematorium. They remain in their homes to receive the men returning after they have performed the funeral rites. An elaborate feast fastidiously vegetarian will be laid out.

When I am on vacation my mother is "dying" to spend maximum time with me. Should there be a death in the neighborhood which she has to attend she will tell me "Don't go anywhere I will soon be back after *crying.*"

Once I asked how is it possible to cry so often and so long over the death of someone you have barely known.

"Oh that's not difficult. You think of someone you loved who has died."

Sanitary downsides and health hazards in the practice of hugging and crying aside it certainly helped to strengthen the union among friends and relatives in the village.

Words don't line up with their labels. Pacific Ocean is not pacific which means peaceful, calm or tranquil. Greenland is not green. Iceland is not icy.

David Morice

CARPET BOMBING PRESCRIBED BY SENATOR TED CRUZ

In December 2015 I heard Senator Ted Cruz, Republican from Texas say in Iowa imperiously with his usual flourish and in staccato rhythm, "we will utterly destroy ISIS. We will **carpet bomb** them into oblivion. I don't know if sand can glow in the dark, but we are going to find out."

Shudders went up my spine when I heard those words. How could anyone who aspires to be president of the United States of America and leader of the free world be so cavalier about killing indiscriminately innocent men, women and children who have committed no crimes? That's what exactly would happen in a carpet bombing!

My thoughts reached back to the time of the Second World War, incidents burned into my childhood memory. I was in Sentul, Malaysia when the British were attempting to take back the country from the Japanese. Our family lived within a mile of the Central Workshop where large numbers of locomotives were housed and the Brits were aware ammunition too was being stored.

The Brits were determined to put the Central Work Shop close to our home out of commission. Mostly in the nights the B 29 Superfortress would target the workshop and although they exercised extreme care very often they missed creating havoc among the civilians. Many innocent lives went under the rubble. We lived day by day in abject fear.

And now I witness a senator, extremely talented and erudite who had not donned a uniform or been in a situation I have been with heartless insouciance promise to carpet bomb an entire city. It's frightening to know there are men who are willing to kill and maim with a tranquil conscience.

I pen it for the relief of my own mind not foreseeing whether or not it will ever have a reader.

Charles Dickens

Chance meeting or is it?

(This is how I remember it. My apologies for inadvertent omissions or commissions in my narrative)

I am aware this is no Stanley/Livingston or Ulysses Grant/General Robert Lee kind of encounters.

Never the less chance meetings have changed lives.

Dogberry's watchmen accidentally uncover the villainy of Don John and deliver Hero from disgrace and death. (*Much Ado About Nothing*)

In "As You Like It" a chance meeting with a hermit results in the sudden conversion of the tyrant Duke Frederick who then easily gives back the throne usurped from his brother.

And this "chance meeting" turned out for my family to be a pleasant happenstance. From this meeting a lasting friendship took root, blossomed and bore fruit.

I was Chief Accountant of The National Trading Company (N.T.C.) in Freetown Sierra Leone. N.T.C was the first public corporation formed with government and public company equity. N.T.C had the sole monopoly for the importation and distribution of basic items of food such as onions, milk, sugar, coffee, tea, tomato paste and so on.

The Barclays Bank of Sierra Leone a British bank was across the street. I walked over to the bank as I had matters to discuss with

Ford the general manager. While I was there waiting to be called I see a young man at the far end of the hall. This is a game I play. Try to guess a person's nationality. I contain my curiosity and refrain from asking as is often a habit with folks in the United States times when curiosity gets the better of good breeding, "Where are you from?" This question is posed as a rule to those whose accent is palpably foreign. So long as you do not utter a word you will be spared of this indelicate invasive probing. I have never once been asked brusquely "where are you from" by strangers in any of the many countries I have lived in.

My office cubicle had a glass front partition beyond which was the accounts department. From where I am seated I could see foreign nationals walk into the accounts department and make inquiries from my staff and then come over to see me. I would tell myself this must be an Englishman and it turns out to be a Frenchman. A Frenchman will turn to out to be Dutch and a Dutch a Swiss. Ten out of Ten I am wrong.

This young lad looked an Indian. Sri Lankans, Bangladeshis, Pakistanis, they all look like Indians. Just as the Caucasian, the Mongoloid, the Negroid, the Pacific Islanders look alike. There are so many Indians in Freetown so another Indian is like coal in Newcastle or a coconut in Sri Lanka. He edged gradually close to me and asked the question that gives me the burr under the saddle every time it is posed. "Are you from Sri Lanka?" he asked. I expect before a personal question is asked one should introduce himself. I replied with unmistakable indifference, "yah" and turned to look towards the manager's office. He continued talking. Described how he left Sri Lanka on a shoe string, his passport was stolen in Turkey (they auction it to Turkish nationals who want to flee the country) he was told where the auction would take place but advised not to be seen there if he wanted to see the sun rise. He narrated with an engaging smile, the way he thumbed his way to France and got a job with a popular French company doing business in Freetown. (*I* noticed *he had a surname which was known among the business community in Sri Lanka.*) I know he recounted many more riveting episodes, sad to say I am unable to recall them now. And that's how he said he ended up in Freetown, Sierra Leone.

This young man was so sincere, affectionate and frank with an irrepressible smile believe me I was completely swept off my feet. Just then I was called. I said "Harold look that there is my office. Come over after I am done with the manager and we will talk."

He did come over and we talked. We both went to our house and there he met my wife and our two plus year old daughter and had lunch. From this day on he would regularly come over to my office, and we would drop by his company provided bachelor apartment and a gregarious friendship was born.

And then this:

Not long after our first encounter around twelve O'clock "High Noon" Harold came to my office and said, "Chandra I want you to do me a big favor" and continued talking without waiting for a reply. His fiancé is in London and is due in Freetown. He wishes to marry her in a church. "Would I give the bride away?"

Stone the crows! I was completely bowled over. This was in 1973 or thereabouts. Since then my family of three had grown to four with the addition of a son. My wife and I have become grandparents. So much water over the dam!

I did not feel up to the task. I felt a more senior person in age and rank would better fill the bill. And yet he needs help and soon. The bride is in London and would breeze in any time now. There was no time for Shillyshallying. And so I tell him I know a fine Sri Lankan gentleman employed with the United Nations, a Roman Catholic like him who can be persuaded to do the honors.

Harold agreed to this. Daphne arrived from London and left for the church from our house to become Mrs. Christie David. Mr. Vis gallantly agreed to give away the bride and admirably fulfilled the formalities with the dignity and grace it richly deserved.

If anyone tells me arrangements for a wedding can be commenced and concluded without even a single snag however inconsequential, I say to this man "I'll sell you two Brooklyn bridges for the price of one" if you relate to me one."

True to type there was a surprise. In our search for a stand-in-father of the bride we had by-passed a more senior (in rank) Sri Lankan who was peeved at what he took to be an insult. And so at the time of signing the register this gentleman impetuously hit the skids. It turned out as time passed by to be just another tempest in a test tube.

As the Dutch would say "eind goed, al goed" and Shakespeare, "All's Well That Ends Well"

Our two families became close friends.

Harold the wandering restless busy bee gathering more honey on the move migrated to Australia where he set up a thriving auto business in Sidney. Harold and Daphne were blessed with two sons and a daughter and are now happy grandparents.

We have visited them in Sidney and they us in Connecticut. When our son was spending a semester in Sidney he was entertained by this outgoing generous couple.

True it's by chance that we met in the hallway of Barclays Bank in Sierra Leone over four decades ago but then it's by choice that we became friends and continue to be so to this day.

I do not know whether anything ever happens by chance.

"It is one of the blessings of old friends that you can afford to be stupid with them." Ralph Waldo Emerson

The most original of authors are not so because they advance what is new, but because they put what they have to say as if it had never been said before.

J.W. Goethe

How I replaced my stolen hub cap

Early mornings on my way to the gym I see students from a high school nearby park in the Plaza park their shiny Lexus, Infinity or a B.M.W with that careless abandon that is born of confidence in their parents' wealth and worth and scamper across in a devil may care attitude to the school. My thoughts would often flash back to my school days in Sri Lanka.

To get to school I had to take two buses. As the bus is sighted commuters poise and crouch like Carl Lewis readying for the hundred meters sprint at the Olympics and while the bus was still in motion we would break away from the queue and make a dash and hop on. When you said "I have to *catch* a bus" you really meant it. I would then hop on a second bus which would regurgitate me at a point from where I schlepp fifteen- twenty minutes to reach my school.

(*By and by my parents got me a pre- owned Raleigh bicycle*)

Almost to a person bought his first second hand car (meaning pre –owned) only after he landed his first job with a salary sufficient to pay for spare parts and petrol. The car enjoyed a privileged position in a person's total assets. On the status totem pole you were up there. Spit polished and hand washed the car would be shining in the tropical sun round the year. All cars overnight are garaged and bolted.

(On my first visit to London I saw rows and rows of cars parked on the streets all through the night and recall whispering sotto voce "what a country")

I bought my first car a second hand Wolseley 1300 after I got a job as accountant. I did not know how to drive. Someone suggested I take classes in a driving school in Bambalapitiya. It was called **Lionel Learners**. As I enter the office a big banner greets me **"Lionel Learners Live Long."** I paid fifty rupees, cash (big money then) for a four Saturday forty five minute class. I turned up the first Saturday and after half an hour the instructor dismissed me saying he had business to attend, "I will make it up next time" he said and went away. The next Saturday he did not turn up. Neither did he the following Saturday. I gave it up as a lost cause. Took two cardboards 4x4 marked **L** in red ink on both of them, hung one on the radiator, the other on the boot and I was on my way.

The reader must feel bad for me when I say one day when I came up to my car from a spot of shopping in the Fort area I found one hub cap missing. I was very upset. A new hub cap cost a tidy sum those days, days when the importation of cars and parts were restricted. A friend found a way. There's always a way.

He says to me go to this place called Panchikawatte about five miles from home and inquire from one of a row of shops, tiny boutiques really and they are sure to help you. I have never been to this part of the city before. Never had the stones to visit any joint which I felt might be seedy.

So around twelve O'clock noon on a Saturday I set out for Panchikawatte. I was nervous. I had a sneaky feeling it was not legit. Any way I went to this place and looked into the shops. The proprietor like looking man in all of them was very busy transacting business.

Then there was one. Just the owner reading the newspapers. I explained to him in faltering ungrammatical Sinhala that I needed a hub cap. "Let me see" he says. So the two of us and a little boy go up to my car. I show him the replacement hub cap I needed. *It was right rear.* "Fine let's go back to the shop" he says and all three of us trudge to his boutique. He then tells the young fella "Martin" Mahathaya (Master) needs a hub cap - go and get one quick" I think that's what he must have said. I could see the boy open a drawer, pick up a screw driver and set off. The whole thing didn't look kosher to me at all.

While I was seated there nervous Martin came back with a hub cap. The owner hurriedly gave me the hub cap wrapped in newspaper, took ten rupees for it and sent me off. With a mixed feeling of guilt and satisfaction I hurriedly returned home. I parked the car at home went round to open the boot to remove my belongings.

The *left rear hub cap* was missing.

English which can express the thoughts of "Hamlet' and the tragedy of "Lear" has no words for the "shiver and the headache"

Virginia Wolfe in "On Being ill"

HOW I GOT MY DRIVING LICENSE.

This is a country where very little you can get done if you don't have the right "connections" and there is a lot you can get done if you have the right "connections."

Driving around town with **L** boards in front and rear hanging reluctantly by a twine does not give full satisfaction of owning a car. You feel like a new comer to the club who has not paid his dues. You tend to lack confidence. So I set about getting my license. There was a gentleman living down our lane who I was certain would know someone in the motor vehicles department who can get the deed done. He was a good man. All he expects of you is respect and recognition. You have to in short lionize him. You "bullshit" him, and you're done for good.

I go to him and confess that he is the only one who can help me get a driving license and ask him whether he would mind helping me. He thinks awhile and then says to me "Yes I know one motor examiner. Let me speak to him. See me day after tomorrow."

As suggested I turn up at his place on the agreed day. "Yes I have spoken to my friend. He will help you."

I go to the motor vehicles department at the appointed time and date. It was noon. I see a gentleman come out of his office with a file calling out my name. We both walk up to the car and I got into the driver's seat while he settled- in in the passenger's.

I drove for about ten minutes or less. During this drive two things happened which I remember very well.

My car like many during this time did not have turn signals. So if you are turning right you stick your right hand out to indicate you wish to turn right. When turning left you make circular signs with your right index finger and cars following you will understand you will be turning left. He said to me "You seem O.K. Let's go back to the office." I had to retrace the path I came on.

We drive on the left side of the road.

I drive a few yards, seeing a by-road I planned to go a couple of yards down that road and turn round and get on the main road. I began putting my index finger circular sign to indicate I will be turning left. The examiner asked me "why are you putting the circular sign?" I tell him, "I want to turn left"

"Do you see any car ahead of you?"

No

"Do you see any behind you?"

No

"Why are you then signaling?" I remained silent.

"O K Let's go."

I am now on the by-road. I reverse on to the main road.

"No! No! No!" he says raising his voice. You should never reverse on to the main road. You must turn the car round. Let's go to the office."

This was a time of severe import restrictions and you should have "connections to get anything"

This is the dialogue between the motor examiner and I had.

Motor Examiner: "Where do you work?"

"I am chief accountant at Hunters"

"Could you do me a big favor?"

"Sure. What's it?"

"My wife needs a wick for the Falks cooker. For many months she has not been able to use it and at Hunters she was told it was out of stock. Do you think you can get one for her?"

Hunters were the sole importers of Falks cookers and parts.

"I will speak to the manager of the household department. Tell your wife to see him tomorrow."

We arrive at the Motor Vehicles Department.

"You can collect the license." He gives me a date.

As soon as I get to the office I stop at the household department and speak to the manager Albert.

The next morning the Examiner's wife called and collected the wick.

On the given date I called at the department and collected my license.

The author must be humane to the tips of his fingers. Next to his humility, his supreme virtue is his candor.

Ponzi scheme – where a predator preys on a dolt

I was a victim.

While I was working at the Treasury in Sierra Leone every Monday at ten in the morning a few senior officials in the Ministry of Finance would have a meeting with president Siaka Stevens. He was a down to earth practical person. He was not spoilt by higher education. A union worker he worked his way up to the top of the union hierarchy, grabbed power and ruled as dictator. When I visited Sierra Leone after about five years I was informed he died without money or friends. When the swanky British M.G. sports car was out of production I have seen him being driven in one custom made for him. There used to be in his compound on Siaka Stevens Street a helicopter fueled and ready at all times for an emergency take off should circumstances require it.

He would often tell us never dig one hole to fill another hole. Soon you will run out of land.

This broadly what a Ponzi scheme is. A fraudulent operator which could be an individual or organization distributes "dividends" to its investors not from earnings but from new capital bamboozled from naïve investors on the promise of returns much above prevailing market rates. The predator must keep on looking out for fools who will part with their money. This cannot go on ad infinitum. As president Siaka Stevens warned soon you will run out of land. When that occurs you are left without money and your dignity. You begin to ask yourself "how could I have let this happen to me?"

The most vulnerable to the Ponzi scheme are the 501 (c) 2 Tax Exempt Charitable Organizations that are incapable of generating funds for their projects and have to resort to perennial public appeals for funds. They are forever in search of "sugar daddies."

I was associated with one such charitable 501(c) 2 organization that was doing splendid work in Surinam in South America. We would ship used computers, second hand hospital equipment, potent drugs and other useful paraphernalia. I have visited Surinam with the president of my organization and found our gifts being put to good humanitarian use.

It then came to pass. What most charitable organizations dread. While our overheads – rent, staff salaries, cost of utilities and general maintenance kept rising inflow of funds was lagging far behind. To compound our problems further our sugar daddy was losing interest in us and was very slow to loosen the purse strings.

How Ponzi predators like blood hounds sniff out their prey I do not know. Let's call her Mrs. B (not Mrs. Bandaranaike). She befriended our president and dangled the prospect of raking in big easy money if only we would make an initial large down payment. The president did not go along. He resisted for many weeks. Mrs. B kept at it promising good times. She would call several times a day. On our journey to Suriname we transited at Curacao. She tracked him down there and wanted to know when she could expect the money. We had already begun liquidating our investments to meet current commitments. We were in dire straits. We needed money.

On our return the president called me to his office and requested I make arrangements to transmit a fairly large sum of money to Mrs. B's organization. The exact amount I cannot recall. *If I had put up a convincing case that we should not accede to Mrs. B's demand I feel the president would have gone along.* He would have as he had done in similar circumstances informed Mrs. B the accountant is not in favor. I cannot go against his advice. This I failed to do. Thus I became an accessory.

Checks were routinely signed by me. This check I prepared and passed it on to the president. It was "signed, sealed and delivered' to Mrs. B. And that was it. Until I left the organization we never saw even the semblance of a return. A few months thereafter I had bid good bye.

The question I keep asking is this - would I have behaved so cavalierly had it been my own money? Very likely not!

A fool and his money are soon parted. There's a sucker born every minute.

“Most of my research consists of googling in search of factoids that I can distort beyond recognition”

A cultured man is one who cannot remember the sources of your quotations.

Ezra Pound

No Fixed Abode

In May 1958 the Sinhalese majority gave the Tamil minority a sound thrashing. Thugs went from house to house with a voter's list and picked up the Tamils not to give them a free haircut. Wherever the Tamils were in a minority they feared for their lives and property. Many lives were lost and much property destroyed. Like Moses and the Jews evacuated Egypt and headed for the Promised Land my parents emotionally scarred having once been in the propinquity of death and destruction during Japanese occupation of Malaysia in World War 11, along with many others bought a one way train ticket from Colombo to Jaffna, the traditional home of the Tamils and *whomp, whomp, woof, woof* they were away never to cross Elephant Pass again.

Sri Lanka will never be the same. Things would fall apart. The center will not hold. The Tamil minority would no longer feel secure. Their confidence in a unitary form of government will be shattered. Anarchy like paralysis will creep inchmeal over the Sri Lankan body politic. Democracy will be replaced by mobocracy.

I had to find a place to stay and quickly however temporary until suitable alternate arrangements could be found.

Looking back upon that scene in the calm perspective of almost three decades later I ask the question why?

What you are about to read is how *I understand*, giving a wide berth for the fact that age may have diminished my recollections, as to what happened betwixt the days when I arrived in Ceylon from Malaysia in 1948 and left for Sierra Leone in 1972.

I do not expect consensus *of opinion in what I am about to set down. If two individuals standing side by side on a sidewalk witnessing a car accident can come up with varying descriptions of what happened to which the English language has given a name, "Rashomon effect" how can I expect comity in an emotively hyper-charged subject such as the causes that led to the communal undoing of Sri Lanka in May of* 1958. *It is impossible to write about the events without offending some. Somerset Maugham a physician turned writer, a master craftsman of plot and prose has alerted us, "It is very hard to be a gentleman and a writer"*

Ceylon having achieved independence hard on the heels of Gandhi's liberation of India was about to hold her own first parliamentary elections.

I recall there were two major parties. The Tamil Congress which was led by a charismatic leader called Ponnambalam and the United National Party by D.S. Senanayake. The Tamil Congress received its sustenance entirely from the Tamil speaking people of the north while the United National Party from rest of the country predominantly Sinhalese. The *Tamil Congress* by its very name and stance was segregationist.

From genesis, from parliamentary infancy, politics in Ceylon (Sri Lanka) was carved out on communal lines. From now on it was downhill on roller skates.

I would attend every meeting G.G. Ponnambalm addressed in the temple premises in my village. He was an orator without peer. Pitch perfect in diction and delivery he was in the class of Pericles, Mark Antony and Obama. Crowds would wait for hours for him to arrive and he always arrived late which fueled the crowds' restlessness to hear him speak. Mark Antony in Shakespeare's "Julius Caesar" resorts to theatrics: "Bear with me; my heart is in the coffin there with Caesar, and I must pause till it come back to me." Likewise Ponnambalam when his oratory had reached its calculated crescendo would pause at peak, at a point when the people would crane their necks for more, to ask over a hot mike in English for the right word in Tamil. It was fashionable at this time not to be fluent in Tamil. It meant you were entirely English educated which was highly prized by the "Jaffna Man." I went from my village Chankanai to the Jaffna Town Hall to listen to the results of the Jaffna elections when Ponnambalam politically decapitated Mahadeva the sitting member.

I was part of a vast crowd that had come to hear him speak. The crowd screamed out his name. He gave them what they wanted. He jumped up on the roof of a car demonstrating physical energy and thereafter in his comfort zone of verbal mastery delivered an inspirational, impassioned speech. There was unanimity even among those who opposed him with rancor that as an orator he was a class by himself, stood alone and apart, his style to be *sui generis*. At the flood tide of his energy and power he was invulnerable.

Alas like most politicians throughout the history of mankind who go through more phases than the moon, now stuck in the muck of petty divisive communal politics, he could not move - to the next stage. Become a statesman. He, separating himself from his compadre, the Gandhi like Tamil man's "Honest Abe", S.J.V. Chelvanayagam, whose name brings to mind Dickens' luminescent words that must light up the darkest corners of a politician's soul, Ponnambalam settled for, to use a description now in currency, being "part of the establishment." Victim to the wiles of the seductive Biblical Mammon he fell from grace.

Quoth Charles Dickens: "I would rather have the affectionate regard of my fellow men, than I would have heaps and mines of gold." "Stolen Words" by Thomas Mallon

What is written without effort is in general read without pleasure.

Samuel Johnson

THE LEFTIES OF SRI LANKA – WHEN I LOOK AND LISTEN TO BERNIE SANDERS

The evening before the big soccer match between Jaffna College and Hartley College in a practice game a team mate in "friendly fire" stepped on my right arm and fractured it. Soon after, I was brought down from Jaffna to live in Ratnakara Place in Dehiwela.

In unpaved Ratnakara Place sandwiched, let's say coddled by Initium Road and Frazer Avenue along the sea and a playground in the backyard there were about forty duplexes on very low rent. All of them were owned by a Sinhalese who we never saw and whose name we never knew. Barring two families, the Don Michaels and the Gunawardenes the rest of the renters were Tamils. My brother and I lived in one of these duplexes with my mother who had come down from Malaysia to watch over us.

Now in my senescence when I view the times in retrospect continents and oceans away in distance and decades away in time it gives me immense joy to report that the teenagers, boys and girls who grew up in this by no means a silk stocking district have done their parents proud. Bused or biked to college and back, by backbreaking study and persistent plodding they had qualified as doctors, dentists, engineers, bankers and have settled around the globe, from Australia to U.S.A, from Canada to U.K. wherever money could be made.

When I see the crowds that attend Bernie Sanders's meetings and hear him repeat over and over again and again with gusto that ninety nine percent of the population is being led by the nose to their doom by one percent of the population, my thoughts flash back to my heroes of long past. It was not "the best of times" it was not the "worst of times." They were normal times. It was a time when Peter, N.M., Tampoe and Colvin assailed the affluent referring to them as Danapathis and the rest Sahotharayas. It was a time when Abu Fuard, Sethupathy, Serpanchi, Nirmalingam and H.I.K. Fernando lived not only in our hearts but in our eyes. We would have gladly given one eye to be one of them. It was a time when Supramaniam sat side by side with Samarasinghe and copied from each other's answer scripts.

I was swept away by the flash and dazzle and brilliance of the oratory of the Gunawardene brothers, Philip and Robert so full of fire and promise so it seemed. I would sneak out of home after supper and listen to them in the market precincts of Wellawatte and Bambalapitiya. I did not understand what they were saying because they spoke in Sinhala. There were three words they would repeat throughout their fiery oration- Sahodharayah (brother) Dupathminisu (the poor) and Thanapathi – I understood to be a rich man. I didn't need to understand what they were saying. I knew they will be there for me at all times.

In John Steinbeck's classic "Grapes of Wrath" Tom Joad assures his loving mother. Tom Joad is on the run after he murders a man in defense of a friend.

"They sat silent in the –back cave of vines. Ma said, "How'm I gonna know 'bout you? They might kill ya an' I wouldn't know. They might hurt ya. How'm I gonna know?"

Tom laughed uneasily, "Well, may be like Casy says, fella ain't got a soul of his own, but on'y a piece of a big one – an' then –

The mother with loving concern.

"Then what, Tom?"

"Then it don't matter. *Then I'll be all aroun' in the dark. I'll be ever'where – wherever you look. Wherever they's a fight so hungry people can eat, I'll be there. Wherever they's a cop beatin' up a guy, I'll be there. If Casy knowed, why, I'll be in the way guys yell when they're mad an' – I'll be in the way kids laugh when they're hungry an' they know supper's ready.* ***An' when our folks eat the stuff they raise an' live in the houses they build – why I'll be there.***"

Let no one delude himself that this is pure fiction and therefore lacking gravitas has no merit. Fiction let it be noted is facts in disguise. Shakespeare sourced his plots and characters from historical accounts and classical texts. To name a few, "All's Well That Ends Well", "Cymbeline", "The Two Gentlemen from Verona", "Romeo and Juliet"

We had implicit faith in these lefties. They all had silver tongues by which they charmed a credulous public. Stone the crows! They too became "part of the establishment" - Minister of Finance, Minister of Agriculture, Minister of Labor, N.M.Perera, Philip Gunawardene, T.B.Illangaratne and on and on all of them. They gave up visiting the market precincts of Wellawatte and Bambalapitiya. Wizards at double dealing - while claiming to work for the hoi polloi they feathered their nest. Mired in the morass of bankrupt ideas sans a silver lining, they packed up their loud oratory and bombast, their flamboyant rhetoric full of sound and fury which for a time signified hope, abandoning those who apotheosized them, they followed the tantalizing twins - money and power never to be seen again. Nearly everyone involved had their moments of greatness and moments of unaccountable treachery. You judge a politician not when he is in opposition promising to give away gratis everything like Bernie Sanders, from creation to cremation, but when he is in power at the topmost rung of the ladder. President Harry Truman a politician good and true who should know said:

"You never can tell what's going to happen to a man until he gets to a place of responsibility. You just can't tell in advance."

We will do well to remember "straight trees have crooked roots"

Why should it be so?

The answer may be found in Robert Penn Warren's "All the King's Men"

When the protagonist Jack Burden is ordered by corrupt Willie Clark to get something on the "upright judge"; Burden replies that there can't possibly be "something" on such an honorable man. Willie Clark is not convinced. He believes every-one has a flaw. No human being is perfect. No one is all pure and without some guilt. Go for the skeletons in the closet he is ordered. It is there. **Why will always be there some flaw in us human beings?**

Willie provides the answer.

Willie replies "There's always something. *Man is conceived in sin and born in corruption and he passeth from the stink of the didie to the stench of the shroud, there's always something."*

Willie Clark is right. There's something on the "upright judge" and tragedy results.

Willie Clark to Judge Irwin:

"Dirt is a funny thing. Come to think of it, there ain't a thing but dirt in this God's globe except what's under water and that's dirt too. It's dirt that makes the grass grow. A diamond ain't a thing in the world but a piece of dirt that got awful hot. And God a Mighty picked up a handful of dirt and blew on it and made you and me and George Washington and mankind blessed in faculty and apprehension. It all depends on what you do with dirt."

It is sad in the relentless pursuit of the two traditional metrics of success – money and power – we have debased not only ourselves but even those who must carry our name.

And so when I see and listen to Bernie Sanders and Elizabeth Warren oratorically luxuriating in virginal territory pounding the podium glibly with childish innocence, for now, I say to myself "Dear God I have seen this play many times before."

Dear God the heights to which we have seen politicians rise, the depths to which they fall, the maze of error and avarice and expediency in which they wander over and over again is unbounded by race, religion or region.

A manuscript is like a fetus, is never improved by showing it to somebody before it is completed.

Anonymous

Sri Lanka takes a "left angle" turn

A tender foot that I am, a minnow in fact would describe a "left angle" as the opposite of a right angle. On a clock if 3 O'clock is a right angle then it must follow 9 O' clock must be a left angle. Mathematicians would find this description preposterous. Be that as it may. Sri Lanka took a whopping turn.

Bandaranaike was the heir apparent to the premiership, the presumptive successor to Prime Minister D.S. Senanayake. With masculine impatience and feminine guile Bandaranaike was waiting on the sidelines to don the mantle of premiership when the vacancy occurred. Senanayake while horse riding on Galle Face Green was thrown off the horse and died from the injuries he sustained.

Adam Bellow said "Nepotism is the bedrock of social existence." The premiership went to the son Dudley. Bandaranike slighted, cheated and jaundiced at what had been dished out to him, like all two tongued politicians citing the government's inaction in implementing the official language policies as the real reason formed his own party, The Sri Lanka Freedom Party (S.L.F.P.) Even though exclusively, barring a few hangers on from the Tamil and Muslim communities, patronized by the Sinhalese, in name at least it did not have the under tones of communalism which the name "Tamil Congress" projected.

The day on which Bandaranaike would "crossover" and take his seat in parliament opposite the ruling United National Party

(U.N.P.) was widely reported in the press. It was a day to witness and record in your memory file. I took the bus to parliament and arriving two hours before opening joined the queue. I must have been about number ten. An hour later I was about number twenty. Just before the opening there was no queue. In Sri Lanka a queue is no place for the old. We all crowded at the entrance and as the doors opened rushed in like shoppers at Walmart on Black Friday. Young and athletic I dashed in and grabbed the front row seat in the balcony.

After a while I saw members of the ruling U.N.P. and those who followed Banadaranaike to the newly minted S.L.F.P. enter and take their allocated seats. The balcony was abuzz with excitement awaiting the entrance of Bandranaike. I was going to see history being made. I was on edge.

I saw Bernard Aluvihare, Bandaranike's side kick and faithful lieutenant enter. When a politician who by construction is self-seeking leaves the ruling party forsaking the perks and accoutrements that go with it and crosses over with his mentor willing to chance his political ambitions you then know such a person is truly an ally. Aluvihare occupied the second seat front row away from the aisle. There was polite clapping. The horderves have been served. The gallery was impatient for the main course - S.W. R.D. Bandaranaike. Ten minutes later Bandraranaike walked in. Small in stature (by my recollection) huge in dynamism he was dressed in traditional garb with a blue shawl slung over his slender shoulders. The blue shawl captured the zeitgeist of this emerging nationalist mood and would be copied by increasing numbers in the years to come. The gallery rose to its feet erupting in an ear splitting applause. Bandaranaike bowed to the gallery, to the people whose lives he will change for all time, inexorably and only then to the Speaker. He took his seat in the front row along the aisle next to his protégé Aluvihare. The "left angle turn" had been taken.

In the callowness of my youth, in the exuberance of the moment I realized not nor cared how Bandaranaike will change *all* our lives for the worse, that of the Tamils in particular. Looking back upon it with a deep and sumptuous tranquility of mind from the safe distance of time and place in a mood mellowed by age I firmly believe Bandaranaike committed a crime. He crippled the minds of the people as you shall see.

Good friends are like good books, a perpetual delight

Thirukural

The Missouri Compromise

In the United States in 1819 the state of Missouri requested that as a price for joining the family of states be permitted to retain slavery. It was acceded to and by an act of Congress in 1820 Missouri was permitted to retain slavery.

I wish Sri Lanka had adopted a version of the Missouri Compromise. This way the Tamils in the North and East could have continued to live, enjoy and preserve their traditional way of life and retain English as a medium of instruction in schools. And so much murder and mayhem could have been avoided.

BANDARANAIKE DELIVERS A FATAL MULE- KICK

The two major communities domiciled in Ceylon (Sri Lanka) are Sinhalese and Tamils. The Sinhalese handsomely outnumber the Tamils. In language, custom, religion and demographically the two are divergent. Even in outward phenotype there is dissimilarity. The dissimilarity is deep and pronounced. It is possible to determine from a distance say in a supermarket checkout counter whether he or she is a Sinhalese or Tamil. For many years they lived together like two peas in a pod even though they were in fact two separate peas and poles apart. In the course of time the two peas would morph into two scorpions.

What made it possible for these two very different cultures to live in concord was a common language – the English language. In their homes the native language interlaced with English was spoken. In the class room, in the office, in the playing fields of Royal and St. Thomas, St. Josephs and St. Peters, Ladies or Bridget's wherever the two communities met and dealt and interfaced with the other the common ground on which they stood was the English language, the *lingua franca* which congealed the two communities which had a history of conflict and deadly confrontation in their historical pasts.

The "unkindest cut of all"

Bandaranaike introduced *Swabasha* (native languages) by way of the Sinhala Only Bill to Sri Lanka in 1956. Encouraged by a trusting public largely from the Southern provinces, emboldened by a belligerent Buddhist priesthood, impelled by a shortsighted policy, Bandaranaike short changed, short weighed and short measured a people caught in the swirl of giddy *Appe'Anduwa* patriotism unaware or unconcerned of the irreversible harm that had befallen them. The academic future of all children living and unborn was sacrificed at the altar of opportunism. Bait and switch was complete.

My understanding of the introduction of Swabasha goes like this. Henceforth in schools the Sinhalese will be instructed in Sinhalese, the Tamils in Tamil and off springs of mixed parentage (Tamil-Sinhalese- Burgher-) may be instructed in English if they chose to do so. English was just another subject like Art or Civics or Carpentry.

Bandaranaike prompted by selfish or altruistic motives I do not know but what I do know is by the introduction of Swabasha he deracinated for all time the superior quality of education that prevailed from the pointy peak of Pedrotalagala to Point Pedro, from Batticaloa in the East to Puttalam in the West that was the envy of the neighboring countries. The switch to Swabasha provided a fertile ground in which ill will and mistrust will thrive for children of two different *races* (**no longer now a community**) will develop separately from baby class room to cremation.

Surely Bandaranaike must have known what harm he was doing to his people when he summarily abandoned English for Swabasha - English a language, to quote from my book, "For the Love of Shakespeare," which brought people of disparate cultures from different countries with diverse aspirations, together. From the banks of the Ganges to sacred Lourdes in the foothills of the Pyrenees; from Freetown in West Africa to Murcia East of Spain; from Seoul to Shanghai" and if I may add, from East of the sun to the West of the moon, "you can get by armed with knowledge of English"

Or was he seeing the panoply of history through the narrow key-hole of his day and time, his beliefs and knowledge, the politician's insatiable thirst for power, privilege fueled by a Napoleonic complex?

And so we must wonder again and again and never cease to wonder, would not have Bandaranaike a man of antique majesty and many accomplishments have known the Brobdingnagian consequences of his ill-conceived actions? Politicians' motives are always buried in the fine print and should you fail to read them you will for sure be sold a bill of goods as it happened with Sri Lanka and Swabasha.

Why do I say **"no longer a community**?"

A "Community" is broadly described as "a social group of any size in a specific locality, share government and have a common culture and historical heritage." Its language, and in the case of Sri Lanka, English, that separates man from animal and when you remove language from the equation what you are left with is the animal world in which the numerical minority will be preyed upon by the majority.

The Tamils no longer would have a meaningful share in the government. There never was a common culture. There never was a common historical heritage. What glued the Sinhalese and Tamils was a common language- the English language. The glue now became unstuck.

Is it any wonder therefore that these mischievous and mendacious machinations of the Bandaranaike government reached in the case of the minority community, albeit a model minority the very pits whereas for the majority its magnificent zenith and careened the country the envy of all of South East Asia into the riots of May 1958, the *Kristallnacht* of the Sri Lankan Tamils?

I keep asking those who visit Jaffna the home of my forefathers "How are things now?" Their diffident and somewhat dodgy reply to a man or woman is "You don't have the army there anymore" as if to say everything is copacetic. In my opinion communal friction has not been healed. It has been concealed.

When reading a book, do not dictate to your author, try to become him – be his fellow worker and accomplice.

Virginia Woolf

Off to the Young Mens Christian Association – The Y.M.C.A. of Colombo

With my parents skedaddling off to Jaffna in the throes of the riots of May 1958 and having returned the rented house to the rightful owner I had to find a *home* for my Vespa scooter (the kind you saw Gregory Peck and Audrey Hepburn riding around in "Roman Holiday") a single suitcase and my anxious self.

With inter racial suspicion rife, the army patrolling Colombo streets checkered by checkpoints I did not think it wise to knock on doors to find out whether there is a singles room to rent.

On the urgings of my uncle who knew all the poobahs on the board of the Central Y.M.C.A. I was allowed to stay in the "*overnight*" visitors' room meant for two for *ten days* at the end of which I will have to high tail with my entire earthly possessions - the scooter and single suitcase.

The room I was occupying had two beds and it was meant for overnight visitors only. So why should I be surprised if in the bewitching hour as a matter of course I should hear the key turn and someone turns the lights on, changes into his sarong (pajamas) and seeing the room occupied checks to see whether his overnight bag is locked and settles in.

Why then should I be surprised if in the afternoon when I checked in at lunch time after coffee and sandwich at the cafeteria I saw a new person seated on his bed, look up with affected indifference, measure me up and continue perusing papers perhaps preparing for a meeting he had traveled to Colombo. This life of living charily with a stranger sometimes two a day persisted for the allotted period of ten days after which I moved to a hostel on 676 Galle Road.

During this layover at the Y.M.C.A. hostel I a juvenile still wet behind the ears by far a Young Man and not a Christian by a long shot can recall two incidents.

The rule that was religiously observed with penalty of summary expulsion was no consumption of liquor in the premises. You may come in after work tanked and befuddled but no imbibing within the four walls.

1. There was a large room with about ten beds and occupants would place their belongings in a trunk which would be shoved under the bed. The bath rooms were along the corridor. It was well known that this dude no sooner he woke up each morning would pull the trunk from under the bed take a bottle out and have a quick shot of arrack. Only then will he open his eyes fully for business.

The secretary of the Y.M.C.A. was determined to nab him in the act. One morning he walks into the room and (call him Jay) sees Jay take his bottle out of the trunk. "Aha" he thinks I've got him. Jay with poise and detached indifference to Lenny looking down on him opens the lid of the bottle containing arrack pours some in the hollow of his left hand, applies it on his head, closes the bottle tight places the bottle in his trunk, pushes it under the bed and walks off to the bathroom down the corridor perhaps humming "catch me if you can." Secretary Lenny confirmed this incident at the farewell party given to him.

2. In the lounge I noticed a guy in the evenings dressed to the nines and was curious to know who he was. And this was told to me.

He was a resident at the Y.M.C.A. There was a hotel called the Galle Face Hotel close to the "Y". This gentleman would scan the morning papers and should there be an announcement of a wedding reception at the hotel he will go there and have a good feed, come back and boast to his friends. He was never challenged as neither bride nor groom was certain which side had invited him.

I am a writer who doesn't belong completely to any language.

Jumpha Lahiri – "In Other Words"

THE SINHALA ONLY POLICY AFTER SHOCK

Parents soon realized substituting the native languages for English as the medium of instruction in schools would place their children at a huge disadvantage when competing with their peers educated outside Sri Lanka. What then can be done about it? Send them to the United Kingdom where they could receive a sound education, mostly in the medical and legal professions and on their return will be assured of landing plumb positions.

I saw wealthy Sinhalese and Tamil parents and even politicians of leftist persuasion, those of the "Sahodharaya" club pack off their children to the United Kingdom. I saw them come back and lord it over the Sinhala stream/Tamil stream educated kids whose knowledge was paltry and their self- confidence abysmal. I saw professors, engineers and technicians flee the country and take on jobs overseas even if it were not entirely to their liking. My friend Mano a banker who accepted a position with a British bank in London was told at the time of hiring that he will be working in the backroom away from public gaze.

The burlesque aspect of what was being played out is that the majority of Sri Lankans, Sinhalese and Tamils either for lack of resources or resourcefulness accepted the new order with neither whimper nor whine.

I bear no ill will against those who sent their children overseas for an English education. Parents will bend, break and even make new rules if it would help their children.

A flinty, implacable bull headed Republican like Dick Cheney took a pass on the "sin" of Sodom and Gomorrah only because his daughter was afflicted by the "love that dare not speak its name."

In Kings 3:16-28 do we not see when wise Solomon ordered the child split into two the real mother in anguish agreeing to drop her claim just so that her baby may live?

There is even a scientific explanation for this. Robert Martone in "Scientists discover children's cells living in mother's brains" writes, "The link between a mother and child is profound, and new research suggests a physical connection even deeper than anyone thought."

I will state simply the umbilical cord of attachment between mother and child is never severed.

My beef is that overnight the *twin scales of fair play and equal opportunity* was tilted in favor of the wealthy. Here's what George J Mitchell former Leader of the senate and architect of the Belfast Peace Agreement says in his book "The Negotiator"

"In America no one should be guaranteed success. But everyone should have a fair chance to succeed."

Sri Lankans were not given a fair chance. The new system guaranteed success for the children of Dhanapathis. The dice was loaded in favor of the wealthy right from the start.

Where was I? I was sadly on the wrong side of the ledger.

The components of good writing:

Lucidity. Simplicity. Euphony.

LIGHTNING STRIKES THREE TIMES

Soon after the war was over father uprooted us from Malaysia, a country of many colors – black Tamils, yellow Chinks and brown Malays and planted us in foreign soil – Sri Lanka with its attendant problems of acclimatization. He was convinced we would benefit from the superior education to which we would have access.

Now with the introduction of Swabasha (mother tongue) as the medium of instruction in schools, parents with professional qualifications successfully snagged overseas jobs and left in a hurry in order to educate their children abroad and those blessed with ample lolly stayed at home and sent their children to the United Kingdom or the United States for a quality education that will no longer be available in Sri Lanka.

We had an eleven month old daughter whose education was paramount but had no patrimony for a back- up. Hobson's choice in these circumstances was to find employment overseas and garner sufficient foreign currency for the child's education. After anxious months of failures and what appeared to be a never-ending series of setbacks with the help of very close friends I had an offer from Sierra Leone which I was hell-bent to grasp come what may even if it meant chucking up a well-paying job as Company Secretary/ Chief Accountant of a leading corporation in Colombo.

I received a call from Sam Kadirgamar Q.C. acting chairman that I should come over to his house for a chat. I believed and quite correctly it turned out to be to dissuade me from resigning as the chairman George Gordon furloughing in Scotland at that time had informed him that I will be made a director of the company. I recall having adequately prepared for the encounter detailing the reasons for my wanting to bolt from Sri Lanka chief among which was that the country was turning autocratic and this country was no place to educate a child. To which he replied if that is the reason for your leaving young man Africa is not the place you should be going to. Little did the good Queen's Counsel know I was using this job opportunity as a jumping off point to migrate to a civilized Anglophone country without politician imposed language barriers where a person may not be guaranteed success but at least to succeed will have a fair chance.

l'homme propose, dieu dispose. Proverbs 16:9 – A man's heart deviseth his way but the Lord directeth his steps.

From Sierra Leone on to Liberia and the coup in Liberia brings us scurrying back to Sri Lanka where the use of Swabasha (National languages – Sinhalese and Tamil) in school was at full blast with distressing effect on our very young school going children. They needed private tuition in Tamil which has become a foreign language to them and to which they did not take kindly. And so once again like stout Cortez with eagle eyes I scan the seven seas for a job overseas – that springboard again.

"There's always" said Graham Greene "a moment in childhood when the door opens and lets the future in" and so it was with our two children. A cable from my good friend Mooly arrives from Sierra Leone suggesting I apply for the post of Accountant General. My application is successful. The lightning for me has struck for the third time. All the important decisions of my life had always been taken precipitately. My anxiety to pack up, the whole pack of us, and leave was in character. A gambler at heart throughout my life I would make monumental decisions entirely on impulse throwing caution to the wind with scant regard for consequences and Heaven forbid should the shit hit the fan then ride out the consequences with giddy abandon. What else can one do?

We pack up and leave and will in due course renounce Sri Lankan citizenship and embrace American which with all the shortcomings of democracy we believe in America the system of checks and balances will always prevail thus preventing the abuse of power we witnessed from the front seats in third world countries wherein savage autocrats spoiled by the adulations of a timid sycophantic public, run amok.

My best friend is a person who will give me a book I have not read.

Abraham Lincoln

The Library, the Librarian, You and I

"My Library was Dukedom large enough"

Prospero in "Tempest" by Shakespeare

"I have always imagined that paradise will be a kind of library." Jorge Louis Borges

There used to be a kindly lady, Elaine, a pseudonym really, who would every time she saw me at the library ask, "Why can't you do your writing at home?" A question for which I could not give an answer that would satisfy her. The telephone, the television, the U.P.S. man, the goodies in the refrigerator, the peanuts at my elbow they all distract me I would plead. She was not convinced.

At high school when I used to be living in the hostel I would tip toe into the library, which justifiably had the reputation of being the best school library in all of Sri Lanka, funded by the American Mission, collect the mail from my parents in Malaysia which would have a dollar or two equivalent and then tip toe out, for the librarian a mousy little man was a devil. Believe me. He could hear the sound of a silent fart. He would come to you and with a flick of his right index finger have you out *now.* If you saw him approaching you, you would be wise to leave in a hurry and save the embarrassment.

From Jaffna I move to Colombo. There were two libraries here both in Colpetty; the British Council on noisy Galle Road and the Public Library along the staid and sober Flower Road. The

British Council library well lit by the Tropical sun had comfortable chairs was ideal for light reading. I would go directly for the very entertaining British "Punch" and other magazines. These were my only windows to the outside world. I would scan the magazines and dream pretty dreams of far off capitals, the "Big Ben" in London, the Eiffel Tower in Paris, of Hollywood movies, John Wayne in "True Grit" and Gregory Peck in "To Kill A Mocking Bird", the Trevi fountain in Rome where we were told if you throw a coin with the right hand over your left shoulder you will surely return, the Floating Market of Bangkok, a boat ride down the Amsterdam canals, Geneva and Zurich, alas all of them beyond my pecuniary reach. What I could not afford in cold cash I could mentally grasp in the sanctum santorum of the silence of the library. In this library you are likely to run into celebrities in the sports, government and corporate worlds. There used to be a notice I recall, in "Jeevesian" humor on the circulation desk – CHILDREN PLEASE STOP YOUR PARENTS MAKING MARKS ON BOOKS.

If you are preparing for an examination and have to put in long hours of study you will go to the cavernous, dim and dark Public Library with long desks and hard bottom chairs. The library opened at eight in the morning and remained open till late in the evening the exact time I cannot recall. A long queue forms well before the library opened for business and as the doors open there is a "food fight" for window seating. You would place books hurriedly in different places thus reserve seats for yourself and for your friends running late. This will hold good for the rest of the day. Friends will have an eye when you step out to grab a bite.

I did not have the same "home" address for more than nine months in a year and there were many like me. They did all their reading, writing and reflecting in the library for when they went back to their box-like room it was to sleep perchance to dream no more. This is not my experience alone. Read the experience of my favorite, the doyen of all librarians everywhere, the Seattle librarian Nancy Pearl the author of the popular, "Book Lust"

"It was painful to live in our house, and consequently I spent most of my childhood and early adolescence at the public library. The librarians at the Parkman Branch Library found me books that revealed worlds beyond what I saw and experienced every day"

And here's Pulitzer Prize winning author of many best sellers, Jhumpa Lahiri on the transformative, nay magical influence of a library, in her book "In Other Words." She like Jacob was wrestling to be proficient in Italian.

"One day I find myself in a library where *I never feel very comfortable, and where I usually can't work well.* There at an anonymous desk, *an entire story in Italian comes into my mind. It comes in a flash. I hear the sentences in my brain. I don't know where they originate I don't know how I'm able to hear them.* I write rapidly in the note book. I'm afraid it will all disappear before I can get it down. Everything unfolds calmly. I don't use the dictionary. It takes me two hours to write the first half of the story. *The next day I return to the same library for another couple of hours to finish it."*

In a library you can lose yourself in fantasies of your own choice, give "voice" to your emotions and imagination undisturbed while in the belly of intense activity. Unlike in the mall or supermarket there are no outsiders in a library. There is a common cause and that is primarily to improve one's mind.

I am often asked what I do all day and I reply "I go to the gym "– this they understand "and then what?" – "I go to the library" – I get a funny look. I don't blame them. There are many who are joyfully ignorant of how much one can get out of a library free, *libre, gratis* without parting with your dignity.

Teenagers who need direction on homework assignments, retirees to read the newspaper obits, book clubs, toddler's story time, cooks looking for a new recipe in a recently published cook book, DVDs and audio books for all ages, a cool place in the heat of the summer and a cozy warm place in punishing cold winter, a haven for the idle and rudderless to while away part of the day, people looking for peace and quiet for a while, help in the preparation of end-of-year taxes, lonely people looking forward to interaction with fellow patrons, writers trying to find ways to get their books published, access to computer, online searches, printing and copying. The facility I have benefited most is the access I have to all the libraries in the state. If you need a book on any subject very likely it would be in one of the libraries in the state and your local library will track it and bring it "by the ear" for you.

The benefits I have listed are just a snippet of what is out there waiting to be taken advantage of.

Scott Sherman in his book "Patience and Fortitude" recounts Senator Patrick Moynihan's experience at the Public Library on 42nd Street, New York:

"Senator Daniel Patrick Moynihan who had toiled as a boot black in Time's Square in the 1940s recalled, "It was the first time I was taught that I was welcome in a place of education and learning."

Pray what a difference it had made to the life of this saintly senator from New York. Senator Moynihan's initial irrational animus towards libraries is quite understandable. There are many who believe the library is an enclave for bibliophiles, nerds and bookworms. This may be why recently I saw a very young Afro –American walk nervously into the library, timorously approach the long desk at which I operate and with trepidation boot- up his lap top and got to working with swift fingers on keyboard and eyes wholly on the screen. I could see he was not comfortable in this environment. Whenever I see a lad engaged in studies unsupervised making a sincere effort to better his position my heart goes out to him. I would have been playing cricket with likeminded buddies. And so on the second day without being nosy while leaving I said to him "Whatever you are doing man I wish you well." He beamed. He smiled from ear to ear and said "Thank you sir. I am applying for colleges." He must have felt he now had a seat at the table.

The library is a people's institution where a senator, a scholar and a dumpster diver is welcome with equal enthusiasm to breathe the same intellectual air. Janice James in "The Wonderful World of Books" puts into words what we who use the library continue to experience and come to expect.

"I've traveled the world twice over,

Met the famous saints and sinners,

Poets and artists, kings and queens,

I've been where no one's been before,

Learned secrets from writers and cooks

All with one library ticket

To the wonderful world of books."

Nobel laureate Jean-Paul Satre encapsulated the above sentiments in one sentence – To him "The library was the world caught in a mirror."

Karl Marx wrote his most celebrated book "Das Kapital from within the confines of the British Library housed in the British Museum. Alex Haley did his research for his controversial "Roots" at the British Library. Christine Marie Peto I am aware spent long hours at the British Library to produce the impressive "Mapping and Charting in Early Modern England and France"

Author Jane Resh Thomas states "We should cut library services for children no sooner than we shrink the fire department, and give new mothers library cards in the obstetrics wards and promote the delight of reading to babies."

The libraries in poorest neighborhoods should be the best in the city. Children who read stay out of trouble and as you are reading you are learning and the more you read the more you want. It's an addiction you can be proud of. Bibliotherapy is more satisfying, more effective and by far cheaper than psychotherapy. One can judge the caliber and class of the denizens of a town by the state of its library. A civilization traduces its library at its peril.

Those who wish to destroy the civilization of a race first commit the crime of biblioclasm by destroying libraries, the temples of learning that serve as sentinels of indigenous culture. It's a tool widely wielded by despots to annihilate a culture anathema to them. Lawyer Raphael Lemkin called such destruction cultural genocide thereby breathing life into books. From very early years Hindus are taught to treat books reverently and by extension learning. Should one accidentally step on a book the perpetrator must ask forgiveness from Saraswathie the Hindu goddess of learning.

Here's what David Baldacci, author of "Escape" has to say about dictators and their uneasiness with libraries:

"Libraries are the mainstays of democracy. The first thing dictators do when taking over a country is to close all libraries, because libraries are full of ideas and differences of opinion, all things we say we want in a free and open society. So keep 'em, fund 'em, embrace 'em and cherish 'em."

Is it any wonder therefore The Library of Congress was burned to the ground by the British during the war of 1812, the Jewish holy books by the Seleucid monarch Antiochus 1V, the Buddhist writings in the Maldives, the Chinese libraries by the Japanese, the Jaffna library in Sri Lanka by the army, the Irish National Archives during the Civil War, the Leftist books in Chile after the 1973 coup d'état, the Leuven University Library by World War 11 German occupation troops to name just a few?

Reading makes me want to write and writing makes me want to read.

Katherine Paterson

THE LIBRARIAN

A library is more than books along the walls and a bank of clicking computers. While the library is the gateway to knowledge the librarian is the guide who will help you to get there. A library without a competent librarian is Shakespeare's Hamlet without the Prince of Denmark. A librarian is not the comic book tweed skirted Toon in high heels who has her nicotine stained finger to her lips saying "shh."

He or she is one rather than knowing everything about everything, can tell you where everything is and help you find it. You ask for A and to your pleasant surprise you will be given A plus something more. The librarian is not just a search engine. The librarian needs to be a search engine with a heart.

A provincial librarian I expect must torment in the absence of microfiche, handicapped by scarce resources – staff and funds - stretch his/her ingenuity to the giddy limit to find shelf space and then as I would be, pained to discard books with a low turnover, cognizant of the fact that these budding authors who will now be relegated to one hop from the dumpster, gave their precious time honing their skill every waking hour, their love of reading and writing to their work of love in the fond hope it will have a permanent home.

Having spent a good deal of my lifetime within the portals of a library in the United States and overseas now I begin to wonder how I would describe the position of the librarian. Is it a job, a career, a profession, a vocation or a calling?

Not blessed with the third eye of Shiva I pawed the internet for help. Here's what I got.

Job: "A job is any work for which you are paid. It can be temporary or long term, part-time or full time. It need not have any expectation beyond the pay check."

Career: "A career is a long-term or lifelong occupation. In other words, it's more than just a job. It's a job with an end goal in mind. Another way to say that is, it's a job with definite long-term benefits and that exceed merely trading work for dollars."

Profession: "A profession is any occupation that requires specialized training."

Vocation: Requires dedication – an indispensable ingredient

A Calling: "An invitation given to men (women) by God."

I wish I will know how the readers would decide.

As for me "Job" is out of the question. A librarian interacts with patrons from kids to octogenarians everyday whose needs and interests are at variance and have to therefore perform beyond the job description.

I will rule out "Calling." – An invitation given by God.

My belief is that it's an amalgam of "Profession", "Vocation" and "Career" – "long term benefits and that exceed merely trading work for dollars" of a career, the "specialized training" of a profession and the "dedication of a vocation"

For a librarian an exemplar I can think of no other than Nancy Pearl the author of "Book Lust." For her becoming a librarian is all she wanted. For her it was very close to a calling as you shall see.

"By the time I was ten years old" she writes in "Book Lust" "I knew I wanted to be a children's librarian, just like Miss Long and Miss Whitehead, the two main influences on my reading life. And although for a few moments in college I was tempted to go to MIT to study transformational grammar with Noam Chomsky, I've never since wavered in my belief that being a librarian is one of the best, and noblest, careers that anyone could have."

Men and Women who gave the soft glow of respectability to the career, profession or vocation of that of LIBRARIAN:

Benjamin Franklin

Golda Meir

Pope Pius X1

David Hume

Lewis Carroll

Marcel Proust

Jacob Grimm

Philip Larkin

Nancy Pearl

POSTLUDE

"All but death can be adjusted" - Emily Dickinson"

Soon gnarled and brittle I shall lie in the lumber room to be coffined, hearsed and cremated and until then I must gracefully take each day as it dawns, exercising, reading, writing and in the reclining chair relax with the remote control.

For all the rapture of life, for all its turmoil's, its anxious desires, it's manifold pleasures and even for its sorrow and suffering, defeats and disappointments with malice to none I bless and praise and thank with all my heart the many anonymous faceless countless friends in three continents who have sans reward helped my family and me to keep moving forward and onward.

"*I can no other answer make but thanks*

And thanks; and ever thanks." Act111, Scene 3 "Twelfth Night"

I let everyone read everything. If they want to. If I know that a novel will offend a certain person, I won't send it to him or her. If people are interested, I hand them out like candy.

Neil Zink

Just what I intend doing.

Home in Freetown along the Atlantic Ocean.

Eagle scout, Girisha responding to a toast

Gaitri planning cross country trip.

Our dear friend Vincent (Queen's Scout) who inspired Girisha to become an Eagle scout.

Gaitri in our Freetown house overlooking the Atlantic Ocean.

From Shelton, CT to Berkley, CA in a Corolla.

Girisha in Amsterdam, returning home from Freetown, Sierra Leone.

American Embassy in Freetown, Sierra Leone. Venue for Green Card interview.

Gaitri receiving an award in Freetown, Sierra Leone.

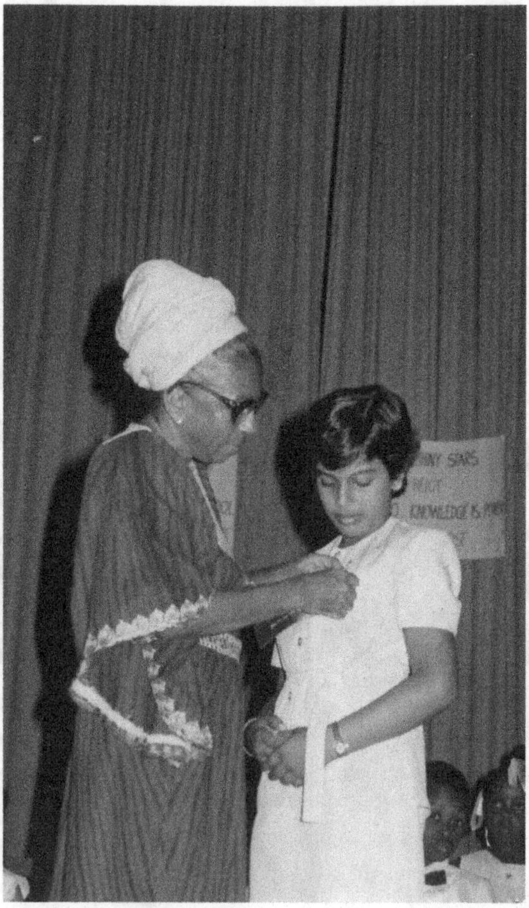

Arrived at Berkley for Gaitri's Master's.

Arrival at Kennedy with Green Card.

The Eagle has landed 33 Kings Hwy Shelton, CT, August 1985.

Excalibur Las Vegas Cross Country.

Family Ensemble

Printed in the United States
By Bookmasters